Exploring
Oral History

Exploring Oral History

A WINDOW ON THE PAST

Michael V. Angrosino
University of South Florida

WAVELAND
PRESS, INC.
Long Grove, Illinois

For information about this book, contact:
Waveland Press, Inc.
4180 IL Route 83, Suite 101
Long Grove, IL 60047-9580
(847) 634-0081
info@waveland.com
www.waveland.com

10-digit ISBN 1-57766-568-6
13-digit ISBN 978-1-57766-568-7

Printed in the United States of America

7 6 5 4 3 2 1

CONTENTS

ACKNOWLEDGMENTS

Oral history is a way of studying social and cultural processes through the collection and analysis of narratives produced by the people who actually lived through the events in question. I was introduced to this research method by my teacher, mentor, colleague, and good friend, the late Julia G. Crane. Together we worked on several projects designed to record the life experiences of people in all walks of life in the contemporary Caribbean, specifically on the islands of Saba, St. Maarten, St. Eustacius, and Aruba. I undertook more specialized training in the methodology of oral history under the guidance of Charles Morrissey, long one of the leading practitioners and advocates of that field of study. I acknowledge my enduring debt of gratitude to both of these scholars.

I acknowledge once again the invaluable support and encouragement of Thomas Curtin, the Anthropology Editor of Waveland Press. Jeni Ogilvie did a superb job of copyediting the manuscript. I am deeply grateful to my colleague Jim Paul of the Department of Special Education at the University of South Florida, who has long been sympathetic to my hopes for introducing narrative-based research in general and oral history in particular to the widest possible audience. Jim and his students in a special workshop on qualitative methods held in the summer of 2006 were most capable and enthusiastic guinea pigs as I was pulling together the material that forms the core of this book.

I want to extend very special thanks to Marc Hébert, gradu-
ate assistant extraordinaire, who made major contributions to the
content of the book and who was always an enthusiastic and
informed sounding board for my ideas.

1

INTRODUCTION
THE CASE FOR ORAL HISTORY

The academic discipline of history is concerned with the description of the people and events of the past and with the analysis of the meaning of those events. The most familiar form of history—the sort we are generally taught in school—relies on written documents archived by governments, private agencies, and scholars. We have been taught to assume that doing history in this documentary manner helps us arrive at the truth about the past. Moreover, since our culture privileges the methods and the language of scientific knowledge, we tend to equate the truth with a compendium of verifiable facts and figures. Literacy is also the basis of our legal, educational, and political systems.

One does not have to be much of a skeptic, however, to realize that we are on rather thin ice if we are dependent on those written archives to verify historical facts. After all, things are collected for a reason, and a common truism holds that history is written by the winners. So much of what remains for the historian to sift through consists of records that history's winners—groups that hold some sort of elite status in society—have thought worth preserving. As a result, the experiences of women, minorities, the poor, those marginalized for whatever reason have rarely made it into the official record. This is not to say that the documents that form the basis of history as we know it are wrong—only that they can only hope to tell one side of a very complex story.

And tell a story is exactly what history does. Nothing could be more boring than a jumble of facts and figures. That they are verifiable may be of some comfort to the scientific mind, but they really do not say much to us unless they are woven together into some form of coherent narrative. Skillful historians are above all master storytellers. History is a lot like life—it is a "test of our ability imaginatively to place ourselves in the positions of other people, so that we can understand the reasons for their actions" (Hoopes 1979:3). But no matter how objective they may strive to be, historians are creating narratives that reflect their own interests, theoretical assumptions, social class, gender, and so on. We must therefore learn to read even the most scientific, apparently objective documentary history with an eye toward the deconstruction of the factors that led the historian to produce a certain story.

Flowing from these general observations, we may state the working premises of the volume that follows.

- History is a created, constructed narrative of past events.
- The narratives of academic history are heavily skewed toward telling stories from the point of view of social and political elites.

If we accept these premises, we might ask whether there is a way to construct history that broadens our understanding of the past beyond the officially accepted master narratives. The answer is "yes," and that way has come to be called *oral history*. We have come to understand that the world is a diverse place and that history, far from being a stately progression of "great men," is really a dynamic set of ever-shifting relationships among groups of people. That understanding was slow to catch on among established scholars of history, and so oral history began as a fringe interest, largely among amateurs. Historians working in societies without significant written archives, where writing and reading were not predominant forms of communication, have long relied on the oral traditions of the people they have studied. Yet the *specific methods* of oral history, as described in this book, did not quickly take hold with professional historians as a group. Oral history has nonetheless become a recognized, vibrant multidisciplinary field in its own right, prized for its ability to welcome the voices of those traditionally ignored by historians to the larger discourse about people and events.

Oral history operates on the assumption that history is all around us and that we all have access to it. It is not the exclusive preserve of the wealthy and powerful. We can, in fact, find it in the living memories and experiences of those still among us. Everyone has a story to tell—some people have many of them. Sometimes this is because they were caught up in some momentous event like a war or a natural disaster. Sometimes it is because they lived through experiences that were mundane enough on their own terms but that seem extraordinary in hindsight because they have for the most part vanished; for example, there are still elders among us who can remember a North America that was largely a rural society with expectations about family life, interpersonal relations, and technology that are extremely different from those that now characterize today's culture. Sometimes people remember stories their own elders told them, so that while there are no longer individuals alive who can recall being slaves in the antebellum southern states, there are plenty of folks whose families have carefully passed on the remembrances of those who did live in those times.

Are any of these stories more accurate or verifiable than the master narratives that have come down to us through academic scholarship? No, since they too reflect the particular points of view of the people who create them. But they certainly give us a bigger, more comprehensive, more complex picture of events and people we thought we already knew. We can think of them as vital, long-lost pieces of the vast mosaic that we call history.

As Barbara Sommer and Mary Kay Quinlan (2002:7) point out, oral history in one form or another has become prominent among several important categories of people beyond academe. Consider, for example, the following.

- *Historical societies,* whether formal government agencies or local grassroots organizations, use oral history as a means to "collect primary source information about a subject either forgotten or neglected by the written record." Because oral history can readily involve people in the community, an oral history project is an excellent way to link the formal organization to the very people whose history that is interested in preserving.

- *Community organizations* such as religious institutions, libraries, schools, or volunteer programs use oral history to document their own activities. Government agencies at the municipal, county, state, regional, and federal levels use the method for the same purpose. (In theory, there is no reason why a truly ambitious international agency could not be added to their ranks.)

- *Families* have added oral history to more traditional means, such as scrapbooks or journals, of documenting the lives of their members.

- *Educators* have come to embrace oral history because it can be a point of entrée to the cultural resources of the community beyond the classroom. Teachers have found student interviewing to be an effective way to motivate learning; one can learn the facts and figures of history from standard textbooks, but one truly enters into the lived human experience by interviewing participants in selected aspects of that experience. The more those participants have traditionally been edited out of the standard textbooks, the more exciting is the process of collecting their stories for the first time.

It is not out of the question that some of the groups mentioned above (especially civic organizations, local businesses, schools, libraries, and historical societies) may actually have some funds to support a worthy oral history project. Radio and TV stations, and perhaps even newspapers and magazines, might also be in a position to support this research in the interest of good community relations. If you are thinking about a project that might entail some measurable cost, you should certainly approach one or more of these sources; the worst that can happen is that they will say "no," although they might well suggest others to ask.

In my own professional career as a cultural anthropologist who specializes in oral history research, I have conducted projects

2

A BRIEF HISTORY

The recording of first-person narratives as a source of historical data is certainly not new. The ancient Greek historian Herodotus made very effective use of the battlefield reminiscences of soldiers in writing his monumental history of the Persian Wars. But for the most part, such material was considered, at best, to be supplemental to the main documentary sources—colorful, but most definitely secondary. In any case, neither Herodotus nor any other historian who followed in his footsteps made any particular effort to record or preserve a verbatim record of what people said. What made it into the record was, for example, Herodotus' edited gloss of what he remembered someone having told him. And, with all due respect to Herodotus, we can only assume that he chose to edit and include only those eyewitness tidbits that fit his own conception of the story he wanted to tell. Oral history, in the sense of an organized activity designed to obtain and preserve the eyewitness accounts themselves, is by contrast a relatively recent phenomenon.

Most observers would point to activities undertaken under U.S. government auspices, particularly the Works Progress Administration (WPA) and the Federal Writers Project (FWP) during the Great Depression, as marking the beginning of oral history. At that time, teams of researchers were sent out to the highways and byways of America to record all manner of "folk life." Although it is likely that this initiative reflected a desire to find gainful (if temporary) employment for bright, young, but out-of-work individuals, it nonetheless resulted in the amassing of a huge amount of material: songs, stories, photos, as well as the sort of things we have come to call *oral history*—the tape-recorded narratives of real folks talking about their own experiences. Once the emergency of the Depression had passed and the country moved on to the crisis of the Second World War, the material collected in the 1930s just sat, largely without having been catalogued; it was therefore extremely difficult to access and use for scholarly—or even popular—purposes.

Then in 1948 Columbia University in New York City established the Oral History Project, which included a center devoted to collecting oral histories, under the direction of Allan Nevins. Nevins, it should be noted, was trained as a journalist although he ultimately became a highly esteemed historian. As a journalist, however, he understood the need to get the "story behind the story," hence his interest in making some coherent sense out of oral material already collected and in developing a consistent procedure for collecting and archiving additional material. By general consensus, Nevins' project was the effective beginning of oral history as a defined and respectable field of inquiry.

Oral history seems like such a logical way to designate this study that we might assume the title to have been around forever; in fact, however, it was actually never applied to the various WPA and FWP projects of the 1930s. There is a charming, if probably apocryphal story about how oral history got its now-familiar name. Louis Starr (1996), whose article on the history of oral history is considered a definitive work, seems to accept the story at face value. Ronald Grele (1996), equally authoritative, pooh-poohs it as a legend. In any event, the term was apparently first used in a 1942 essay in the influential literary magazine, *The New Yorker*; the article profiled a louche bohemian artiste named Joe Gould who claimed to be compiling a never finished oral history of our time. For some reason the phrase captured Nevins' imagination, and by applying it to his own very definitely respectable project, he established it as the accepted label.

Nevins came to appreciate the value of oral history when he was writing a biography of Grover Cleveland. That president and many members of his administration had actually lived long enough to be interviewed by historians and journalists of Nevins' own generation. Nevertheless, no one ever had the foresight to do so, so enmeshed were they in the traditions of looking only to the written archives as the way to study history. Nevins saw this failure as a great historical tragedy. Indeed, he accurately predicted a time in the not too distant future when advances in technology would spell the end of the production of all those diaries and letters that had for so long been the stuff of historical documentation. Such traditional ways to capture and preserve a written record would be rendered obsolete by new technology. He was thinking of the telephone and telegraph, of course, but his insight has become even more appropriate in our own age of ephemeral electronic communication. If the people making the history were no longer going to produce a written record, then it would have to be re-created in the process of the firsthand interview.

Because of his personal interest in the biographies of great men, Nevins devoted much of the early effort of his center to the compilation of lengthy oral autobiographies of notable personages. The emphasis of the center, however, later shifted to what came to be known as the "special project"; that is, a specific event of significance (rather than the life of a particular person) would be re-created through the oral remembrances of those who had participated. The first such project was an oral history of the early years of broadcast radio. Nevins also forged an alliance with the Ford Motor Company and thus fostered the creation of the massive Ford Archives, which resulted in the largest industrial oral history ever produced.

Despite Nevins' pioneering efforts, he remained very much a member of the Establishment, and his own initiatives within the Oral History Project were directed at the lives and works of the rich and powerful. This tendency was due partially to the kinds of funding available to him at the time. Oral history did not break free of those constraints to become a vehicle for giving/lending voice to the voiceless that its enthusiasts hoped for until the 1970s. In the wake of the civil rights movement, the women's movement, and movements directed at the improvement of the lot of people with disabilities and variant sexual orientations, oral history came to be recognized as an effective way to reimagine history with its long-missing pieces restored.

Oral history became a "movement" in its own right, as its proponents developed an almost messianic fervor about empowering the marginalized and hence reconstructing history and de-centering the elitist master narratives that had been part of the received wisdom about the past. Oral history, in fact, became an integral part of emerging academic programs in Women's Studies, Africana Studies, Disability Studies, and so forth (see, e.g., Vaz 1997). Its methods have been enthusiastically adopted by anthropologists and others who study non-Western cultures. A number of best-selling works popularized the genre, most notably the books of Studs Terkel (e.g., 1974,1986, 1993, 1997, 2000), the tireless chronicler of "ordinary" people and their many and varied experiences in the course of the extraordinary twentieth century.

Oral history is an intrinsically popular form of research because the subjects[1] of research are so close at hand. Many people have therefore come to look upon oral history as an agreeable hobby, akin to scrapbooking or journaling. The Story Corps project is currently touring the country; it sets up mobile recording facilities at which "ordinary" people can interview each other for posterity. (See Isay 2007 for more information about this community service project.) While the enthusiasm of such amateurs should be encouraged, it should always be kept in mind that oral history, as a tool of inquiry in social research, requires a good deal more than asking Grandma for her favorite pie recipes. Grandma's culinary skills are certainly one good way to start a meaningful oral history project, but we must always keep in mind the systematic nature of the research enterprise as discussed above so that everyday chitchat becomes the usable stuff of historical research. (See Charlton, Myers, and Sharpless 2006 for a comprehensive overview of the growth and breadth of applications of oral history.)

Note

[1] In recent years, the term "subject" has been replaced by "collaborator," but I have chosen to use "subject" in this text. See chapter 7 on ethics for a detailed explanation.

3

TYPES OF ORAL HISTORY

Broadly speaking there are two forms of oral history research that have been influential in modern social research. Some of this scholarship predates the introduction of the term "oral history," as noted in the previous chapter. The authors discussed in this section used a variety of terms to describe their work, but they all fit comfortably within the definition of oral history used in this book. The first form is associated with European scholars of the late nineteenth and early twentieth centuries, many of them with a Marxist orientation. They were concerned with "the masses" as the agents of historical change and so they subordinated individual stories to narratives emphasizing the collective experience. The early classic in this genre was Thomas and Znaniecki's monumental five-volume study, *The Polish Peasant in Europe and America*, originally published in 1918. As the title suggests, these researchers recorded interviews with rural folk as they were swept up in the great migration from Europe to North America in the decades preceding the First World War. Their study is a comprehensive account of a long vanished way of life in the Eastern European countryside as well as a firsthand account of the collective experience of migration.

Modern oral history projects that focus on putting together a collective portrait of an event as seen by a multitude of participants speaking only about that event (e.g., the recollections of people evacuated in the wake of Hurricane Katrina) follow in this tradition. When it comes to analyzing the results of such studies, researchers have emphasized either the social or the cultural aspects of the narrative. Analysis that focuses on the main institutions of a society (e.g., family, religion, political and/or economic systems) falls into the social category, while a focus on broad themes or values (e.g., patriotism, race relations) are said to be cultural in nature. In practice, it is virtually impossible to disentangle the social from the cultural—the matter of emphasis is one of nuanced distinctions rather than clear-cut categories.

By contrast, American scholars of the early twentieth century tended to focus on particular persons, perhaps echoing the prevailing American philosophy of individualism. This genre, usually referred to as the "life history," can be further subdivided. On the one hand, there are studies that deal with individuals presumed to be "typical" members of their culture, such that the life story of such a representative is, in effect, an ethnography (i.e., a descriptive account) of that culture in microcosm. Among the numerous influential works in this category are Radin's (1920) *Autobiography of a Winnebago Indian* and Simmons' (1942) *Sun Chief: The Autobiography of a Hopi Indian*. These studies are noteworthy for taking readers into the daily lives of Native Americans—people who in those days were thought of in broadly stereotypical terms (either "noble savages" or "bloodthirsty redskins" depending on one's point of view) and rarely in terms of identifiable individuals with lives of their own. On the other hand, there are studies that deal with explicitly extraordinary individuals, on the premise that in such people the aspirations and values of an entire people are writ large.

Some might question how the delineation of a single life could possibly be a valuable resource for social research. Langness (1965:20–31) summarized some of the main reasons for conducting life history studies.

- **The life history helps us understand the structure of culture.** Anthropologists, sociologists, and other social scientists tend to have some firmly held ideas about how social groups are constituted; introductory textbooks in these fields usually divide the world into categories of economics, politics, family life, religion, art, and so forth. These categories make pretty good sense in terms of our own society, but they do not necessarily form an accurate map for everyone. People from other cultures are likely to see the world differently, and even within a single society, there may well be those who for one reason or another do not share the conceptual landscape of others. When people tell their life stories in their own words—the goal of the life history approach to social research—they are, in effect, spontaneously generating their own cultural map. The resulting life story not only provides bits of information about people and events, but the very structure of the story allows us to understand diverse ways of making sense of that amorphous thing we call reality.

- **The life history provides a guide to culture change.** Social researchers of all disciplines are all historians, in the sense that they understand that human social life is never a fixed thing—it is always changing in response to changing stimuli. But culture change is a huge dynamic that is very difficult to wrap one's mind around. If, however, we can see change as experienced by a particular individual with whom we come to empathize through the telling of his or her life story, then the abstract notion of "culture change" comes to vivid life.

- **The life history provides insight into the nature of values.** Other forms of history can tell us about specific events; certain forms of social research are very good at providing statistical support to demonstrate trends and patterns in human experience. But the life history is particularly good at showing us how real people feel about what is happening to them and their social group. It can also illuminate the reasons *why* people have reached those evaluative conclusions about their experiences.

- **The life history is a documentary account of the socialization process.** It is widely recognized that while human beings come equipped with a certain amount of inborn, genetically programmed behavior, the vast majority of what we do is a result of what we learn as we grow up. We are formed ("socialized," or "enculturated," to use the technical terms) because of our interactions with parents, elders, teachers, and so forth—and by our peers as we grow older. Socialization, like culture change, is one of those grand abstractions that social scientists revel in, and it is the life history—the relatable stories of people going through the process of socialization—that takes the abstraction down to the level of real experience.

It should be noted that clinical psychologists use on individual's life history as a kind of case study that sheds light on the individual's problems and suggests means of treatment. Intended for therapeutic purposes, such case studies are generally seen and discussed only in the clinical setting. When case studies are published, however, every effort is made to disguise the identity of the subject; general psychological processes rather than personalized details are the objects of scrutiny. They are therefore not really oral history in the sense we mean here. Another form of psychological case study—the psychoanalytic dissection of famous people—attempts to set extraordinary characters not only in the context of their cultures but also in terms of the psychological dynamics that made them what they were, for good or evil. (See, for example, Erikson 1963:326–358, an examination of Hitler's psychological makeup and its relationship to German national aspirations, and Mandelbaum 1973, an exploration of the life story of Gandhi as a guide to the political philosophy of nonviolence.)

There is little methodological difference between collective oral histories and individual life histories—the main distinction being the unit of analysis: the group or the individual that is the subject of the narrative. Although this distinction is not a trivial one, it can be set aside for our purposes in this text; for the sake of convenience we will therefore refer herein to both event-based and individual-based research as oral history. It should also be noted that when either form of oral history becomes part of the public record (as in a museum display or a library-based archive open to the general public, or when it is used by some sort of political or social group as a way of advancing its own agenda) it is referred to as "public history" (see, e.g., Frisch 1990). That label, however, refers only to the function of the end-product of a project, not to its underlying conceptual basis.

One final term may be added to the profusion of labels introduced in this chapter: the "oral tradition." This term is used (primarily by anthropologists and folklorists) to refer to the body of knowledge (e.g., riddles, satire, prayers, poems) passed verbally from one generation to another in nonliterate societies (Vansina 1996). There are obvious similarities between the oral tradition and the material collected by oral historians, but the terms should not be used as if they were synonyms. Oral history, as we have defined it and as it is used in the rest of this book is practiced mostly in literate societies as a way to supplement the written materials that are on the historical record. Oral history focuses primarily on the firsthand recollections of the people who are interviewed; while they may certainly draw upon an oral tradition (as in the case noted earlier of contemporary African Americans relating stories about the time of slavery that have been passed along in their families), the research strongly favors what they themselves have experienced. (See Dorson 1996 for a more detailed discussion of the relationship between oral history and studies of folklore.)

4

THEORETICAL ISSUES

The most important philosophical debate in the oral history community concerns the accuracy of the recorded data. Although it is now widely taken for granted that even traditional written documentary sources are the products of highly selective bias, oral materials still labor under a special burden of proof, if only because they are so patently the products of individual memory. Oral historians who want to be taken seriously as researchers (and not just as amateur enthusiasts) are therefore very concerned about establishing both the reliability and the validity of their data. These terms reflect a bias toward objective—usually quantifiable—data and are matters of some contention among qualitative researchers in general, not just oral historians. The problem is that establishing statistical reliability is a straightforward enough process when working with numerical data; it is quite another matter when dealing with narrative materials.

Reliability in the oral history context is a measure of the consistency with which an individual will tell the same story about the same events on a number of different occasions. *Validity* refers to the degree of conformity between the reports of the event and the event itself as recorded in other primary sources (e.g., documents, photographs, diaries, letters, newspaper accounts). There is no reason why a research project could not be set up in such a way as to build in several iterations of the narrative (to establish

19

reliability), but the researcher must certainly be aware of the possibility of annoying or even alienating the respondent by asking him or her to repeat the same story several times over.

It is certainly standard practice to embed oral histories in collections of other kinds of archived, documentary history, but doing so merely acknowledges that *all* forms of historical data need cross-referencing, the reinforcement of conclusions by reference to multiple sources (a methodological procedure commonly referred to as *triangulation*). Indeed, Alice Hoffman (1974:27) concluded a very thorough review of the literature on reliability and validity with the limp affirmation that oral history is "simply one among several primary resources. It is no worse than written documents." It is doubtful that anyone updating her review today would reach a more strongly worded conclusion. Most oral historians would probably agree with the assessment of William Moss (1977), that we simply need to be more precise in documenting the circumstances of the research and not just the results of the interview itself.

Doubts about the reliability and validity of the interview itself, however, are compounded by questions about the most common by-product of the research—the written transcript. Even the most accurate transcript really cannot—should not—capture "everything." Every discourse, even if produced by a highly articulate speaker, contains an inordinate number of "hmms" and "uhs" and similar awkward pauses. In ordinary conversation, few people speak in fully formed, perfectly grammatical sentences. A totally accurate transcription would faithfully reproduce every last one of these foibles, thereby making just about every oral history subject ever recorded seem like a bit of a fool. As such, no one expects a transcript to be faithful to the extent that it includes all the hemming and hawing; judicious editing for grammatical coherence is also accepted practice, as is giving interview subjects the opportunity to review transcriptions of their interviews. In my own experience, most subjects are inclined to edit out whatever solecisms remained, even after the careful redaction of the transcriber. On occasion, however, I have encountered people who insist that they want to go on record "sounding like I really sound," even at the risk of being incomprehensible.

But there is a more important problem lurking in the process of transcription, namely the inability of the written word to capture nuances in tone of voice, body language, gesture, and so forth. Such nonspoken expressions often carry a great deal of meaning, most of which is lost in transcription. For example, one of my mentally retarded storytellers noted at one point, "I had a great family." A plain transcription would lead the reader to think the narrator had had a positive experience. But in fact the words were spoken in a tone that was dripping with angry irony—he wanted to convey the idea that he grew up in a family setting that was far from ideal. Since he did not get around to the particulars of the abusive relationships that characterized his family until much later, the remark in transcription would be quite misleading. One could, of course, add "stage directions" to the transcript (e.g., "said in an ironic tone of voice") but then doing so is adding a layer of interpretation to what purports to be a straightforward record.

At best, even the most faithful transcription is an approximation of the spoken discourse; it can never be a completely satisfactory substitute for it, although some people persist in treating it as if it were the only acceptable outcome of an oral history project. Those who use oral history collections primarily for research (rather than for the ordinary pleasure of hearing people's stories) almost always work from transcripts, as if they were more reliable than the recordings themselves. We do, after all, live in a culture that is overwhelmingly literate—we rely on the written word and tend to distrust anything that is not written down. This lingering mistrust of orality is one of the great philosophical paradoxes of the oral history movement.

When oral historians discuss their reservations about standards of reliability and validity, they do so on two main grounds. First, they make common cause with qualitative researchers in general, pointing out that narrative materials are not like the quantified data for which those standards were originally developed. In other words, they point out the near impossibility of devising accurate measures for narrative materials that would allow for the clear-cut statistical computations that characterize analyses of reliability and validity among quantitative researchers. Second, they couch their reservations within the context of a more general caution about memory. There is a large body of literature on the complexities of the psychology of memory (see, for example, Thompson 1988:150–165 for one of the first critical reviews of this literature as it pertains specifically to oral history). On a simpler level, we all know from personal experience that we forget things as time goes by—or that we tend to remember the stories we retell about our experiences better than we recall the original events.

Our recollections of people and events—and our evaluations of those things—may change over time. The story I would tell about my youth in an ethnic enclave neighborhood in a big city would come out one way if I told it at age twenty-one, when I was preparing to go out into the great big world beyond the neighborhood; it would be a very different story if I told it now at the age of sixty when I have grown nostalgic for the scenes of my lost youth. Personal memories may be colored by experiences beyond ourselves; for example, even after so short a time I am hard pressed to separate what I actually remember about September 11, 2001, from what I "remember" from innumerable images of the events of that day that I have digested from TV, magazines, and the Internet over the past several years.

Moreover, when we are collecting an oral history of an event, we must be alert to the probability that multiple observers of the same event will have different recollections of what happened—the so-called "Rashomon" effect, named for the classic film in which each of several eyewitnesses to a crime recounts the story in a different way. Sometimes the differences are those of nuance or emphasis, but more often than not they result in dramatically varying assertions of fact. Even detectives on TV crime shows have learned to be leery of eyewitness accounts, preferring the supposedly more conclusive "forensics" such as DNA. Valerie Yow (2005:35–67) provides a comprehensive overview of the current status of the psychology of memory and its implications for oral history research.

Compounding these normal glitches in the memory process are factors of more or less deliberate deception or dissimulation. No less than the high and mighty letter writers or diarists of an earlier era, oral history subjects today are not above using the interview to grind their own axes. Most people tend to want to burnish their own reputations by remembering their stories in the most flattering possible way. Of course, there are also some people who delight in self-abnegation and who therefore see their past in an unduly harsh light. People may recall events in light of their own psychological limitations, political inclinations, or feelings of peer pressure. And, to be sure, some people simply enjoy telling whoppers just to see if they get a rise out of the person they are talking to.

Two very prominent contemporary memoirists have become objects of controversy because of these problems. The Nobel Peace Prize-winning Guatemalan indigenous rights activist Rigoberta Menchú has been accused of fabricating parts of the autobiographical tale she told to a European interviewer (a book that became an international best-seller) in order to magnify the trials and tribulations of her people (Menchú 1984). She was, in the end, given a bit of a pass because her story had gone through so many levels of redaction and translation before publication that it was impossible to say where the perceived "distortions" had come from. She was, for example, accused of having exaggerated the accounts of soldiers raiding her village and rounding up or killing the people. Some, but not all, of her critics were probably responding from a conservative political position that led them to be suspicious of claims of indigenous rights, especially at a time when political analysts of that persuasion were concerned about the rise of revolutionary movements in Latin America. Since the basic truth of her story—the long-standing oppression of indigenous people in Central America—was not in doubt, establishing the literal veracity of each and every anecdote became a less pressing matter.

On the other hand, the reformed drug addict James Frey incurred the wrath of his onetime patron Oprah Winfrey—and her legions of devotees—for embroidering on his experience when under the influence. It became apparent that he was not as far gone in addiction as he claimed; a number of his accounts of drug-induced feelings or actions were more literary than factual in nature. In this case, Winfrey's patronage had been based on what she took to be the searing truth of Frey's memoir (2003), and it was withdrawn when it was revealed that his book did not fully meet the canons of either reliability or validity that seemed to be required to establish the factuality of his self-portrait. In sum, while the memoirs of Menchú and Frey were not collected as part of oral history projects in the strict sense, they both represent the problems raised by the vagaries of memory. Menchú may have exaggerated some facts, but since she did so in ways that affirmed the political sympathies of most of her readers, her story was not cast aside. Frey, on the other hand, exaggerated in ways that ignored (and almost seemed to mock) the expectations of his audience, and so he became an object of ridicule. The fact is that all storytellers exaggerate; the crucial difference is the nature of their interaction with their audiences.

As this book goes to press, two more examples of faulty memory have hit the media. *Love and Consequences* by Margaret B. Jones is a narrative of a young woman caught up in the Los Angeles gang culture; the author turns out to be Margaret Seltzer, a middle-class white suburban woman. *Misha: A Mémoire of the Holocaust Years* by Misha Defonseca, was actually written by Monique de Wael, a Catholic not a Jew, who was in any case a toddler who was more or less safe at home and not a teenager on the run from the Nazis during the war years. Both of these narratives are complete fabrications and are thus more deliberately deceptive than the merely creative embroidery of Menchú or Frey. But both are well written, compelling books that probably would have been acclaimed as important new literary works had they only been marketed as fiction. As usual, however, our culture's preference for "truth" led both Seltzer and de Wael to try to pass off their made-up tales as factual history.

These difficulties have led some practitioners of oral history to throw up their hands and claim that oral history really is not research at all but is a form of "archiving" sensitive only to the "memory claim" model—recording only what people tell them, the reliability or validity of which is irrelevant. As such people see it, the fact that Mr. Jones includes in his life history a lengthy account of having been abducted by aliens is important in its own right—it is his memory (or his memory as he chooses to report it), regardless of what we think of the likely factuality of the tale even if such unchallenged dubious points call into question the accuracy of everything else Mr. Jones has to say. Oral historians of this persuasion use this argument as a way to avoid submitting themselves to institutional review boards, which oversee the ethical component of research conducted at universities and other research institutions; since what they are doing is not really research, they say, all ethical problems immediately evaporate— their collections are a form of literature, not scholarship.

The speciousness of this ethical claim will be addressed in a later chapter, but in my view it also represents a creative failure of interpretation on the part of some segments of the oral history community. Consider, for example, an experience in my own research, specifically a project based on Saba, an island in the Netherlands Antilles. One of my informants was an elderly black lady who had led a most adventurous life quite out of keeping for someone of her gender and color in her generation. After I returned home, I was sent a copy of the island's newspaper, in which this lady had given an interview to a local reporter. Although most of the "facts" were the same in both accounts, they were really quite different stories.

The tone she adopted with me, a supposedly high-status white outsider, was markedly different from the way she talked to the "local boy" reporter. There were numerous differences in points of emphasis, and it was quite clear that she had omitted some details with me that she included in the newspaper account, and vice versa.

For example, in telling her story to the reporter, she highlighted anecdotes about how she would stand up for herself and not allow herself to be pushed around by her (white) employers. It is not unreasonable to infer that she wanted to convey to a younger generation the idea that the traditions of subservience and deference were not necessarily admirable. When she related those same incidents to me, however, she did not make mention of her attitude of calculated defiance; rather, she stressed what she probably thought I would consider positive traits—her desire to use the money she earned in domestic service to see more of the world and to have "adventures." Moving often from job to job therefore was in the reporter's version a narrative of discontent with the colonial system of stratification (her employers consistently failed to treat her with sufficient respect, so she had to quit); in my version it was a narrative of an adventurous spirit who took advantage of every possible opportunity to learn and grow. The two narratives are certainly not incompatible with one another. My point is simply that all narratives are inevitably shaped and shaded in order to connect with a storyteller's perceived primary audience.

Was she a liar? Was she simply an old lady with a wavering memory? I came to the conclusion that neither of these explanations would do. I realized that like any storyteller, she was gauging her effect on her audience. Without making a conscious effort to manipulate either the reporter or me, she simply adjusted herself and her narrative style to fit the responses she was getting. By comparing the two stories, it was possible to understand a great deal about race and class relations in postcolonial society; such larger insights were just as important as the specific details of local history that were embedded in her stories. In effect, she was not a "reliable" purveyor of "valid" historical fact, but both her stories were true, once allowance was made for the symbolic nature of the interactive space between her and me and between her and the reporter. (See Angrosino 1989b for full account of this matter.)

Consider as well my research among adults with mental retardation living and working in a community-based program. In a desire to learn about mental retardation as it is experienced by people so diagnosed (as distinct from what we know from the clinical literature), I collected life histories from about two dozen clients, putting their encounter with one particular service agency in the context of entire lives lived with stigma. In many ways the results could be considered worthless; the respondents were often not verbally adept and their use of language was disordered, sometimes (but by no means always) to the point of unintelligibility. Moreover, much of what they told me was patently counterfactual—it failed even the simplest, most commonsensical tests of validity, either because their memories were faulty or because they had been socialized into an institutional culture of self-concealment. But I came to understand that important information was conveyed by the style in which the narratives (disordered though they might be) were told and that the respondents' use of the mechanics of storytelling in our culture spoke the truth about their lives and experiences even if they used those mechanics to say things that were not literally factual. For example, one of my storytellers insisted that he was the son of the wrestler Hulk Hogan. I suppose this claim could have been empirically validated, although I doubt that Mr. Hogan would have been inclined to submit to a DNA test just because I asked him to do so. In any case, the far greater likelihood is that my informant was making up the story. Did he do so because his mental disability led him to misconstrue or misunderstand "reality"? Was he merely trying to make himself seem more important by linking himself to a celebrity? Was he simply trying to pull my leg? All of these interpretations are reasonable. But whatever his ultimate motive may have been, his insistence on his relationship with Hogan was the central, organizing metaphor of his narrative. He saw himself as a strong, assertive, heroic figure (despite the evidence of his downtrodden life so obvious to others), and his claim of a relationship to Hogan was his way of symbolizing his self-image. (See Angrosino 1992, 1994, 1997, 1998a, 1998b for further discussion of this project.)

Self-concealment to the point of deliberate deception also figured in my oral history of the monastery, although in that case I have suggested a different psychosocial mechanism that explained the monks' behavior that allowed me to understand the emotional truth behind the superficial misdirections of their narratives. The monks, I believe, were deliberately engaged in concealment because my interviews were among the very few encounters they were allowed to engage in that were not totally constrained by their vow of obedience to their abbot. They were, in some ways, like children suddenly freed from adult supervision; in other words, they lied to me because they could get away with it. But what they concealed (e.g., matters having to do with their psychosexual adjustment to living in an isolated community) was as revealing as what they actually said. (See Angrosino 2004 for a discussion and analysis of the monastery project.)

In sum, I am willing to extend to the likes of James Frey the benefit of the doubt; it is quite possible that his memoir is "true" in a metaphorical sense to the experience of a drug addict, even if descriptive details have been rearranged or distorted in ways more compatible with literary fiction than with social science. This argument will, I presume, not be convincing to those who believe that only statistically reliable and valid conclusions are "truthful," but I hope it will be taken seriously by those who understand that there are many ways beyond the scientific to gain an understanding of the human condition.

Augusten Burroughs is another best-selling memoirist famous for recounting his past life as a dysfunctional multisubstance abuser. Criticized in some quarters for "inaccuracies" in his first autobiographical book, *Running with Scissors* (2002), he made a point to preface his second memoir, *Dry* (2003), with an author's note: "This memoir is based on my experiences over a ten-year period. Names have been changed, characters combined, and events compressed. Certain episodes are imaginatively recreated, and those episodes are not intended to portray actual events." If this admission results in a shift in Burroughs' position in Barnes & Noble from "non-fiction autobiography" to "literary fiction," will that label diminish the powerful—and painfully funny—emotional truth of the story that won him an admiring audience in the first place?

The travel writer J. Maarten Troost takes an even more irreverent stance on the whole matter of truth and fact. In a disclaimer prefacing his book *Getting Stoned with Savages* (2006), he writes, with tongue presumably deep in cheek: "The author acknowledges that he is not Bob Woodward. Mr. Woodward is scrupulous with names and dates. This author is not. Mr. Woodward would never suggest that something happened in October when, in fact, it occurred in April. This author would. Mr. Woodward recounts conversations as they actually occurred. This author would like to do that, but alas, he does not excel at penmanship and he cannot read his notes. However, the author has an excellent memory. You can trust him." Prospective scholarly researchers are hereby warned not to take Troost as a role model when proposing projects, requesting money from funding agencies, or publishing the results of research.

What relevance do the misadventures of Menchú, a globally known political figure, or of Frey, Burroughs, or Troost, sophisticated professional writers, have to do with "oral history"? Surely, one might think, ordinary people are incapable of the sorts of cleverly imaginative recreations that are the stock-in-trade of published authors. Think again. "Ordinary people" may not be able to turn a phrase as elegantly as a pro, but are their motivations really so different?

I believe that we do ourselves a disservice if we try to link "truth" and "verifiable fact" too uncritically. "Truth" comes in many guises. The truth conveyed by a great poem is certainly different in form and style from the truth as conveyed in a scientific monograph, but one is not inherently inferior to the other. Nevertheless, if we want to make sure that oral history is indeed taken seriously as research, we cannot play the "poetic" card to exclusion. We must be mindful of some very basic steps we can take to insure reliability and validity in our methods that even skeptics can appreciate. To do so, we can do no better than to follow the advice of Moss (1977), who suggests that we evaluate the content, conduct, and product of oral history.

When we evaluate *content* we strive to insure that the narrative is corroborated by other sources whenever possible, that the interviewer considered alternative interpretations of the story (and did not get hung up on just the interviewer's or the subject's pet peeve), and that, to the extent that the narrative challenges the received wisdom, it does so in a responsible fashion allowing for reasonable discussion (i.e., it is not simply an intemperate rant).

When we evaluate *conduct*, or the method by which an interview is conducted, we must remember that an interview is not a passive process by which an interviewer is simply a neutral receiver of whatever he or she is told (as in the memory claim model); in fact, the interviewer is engaged in a conversation—sometimes confrontational, but always dialogic in nature—with the subject. So we must try to ascertain whether the interview was itself conducted in a professional and responsible manner, regardless of what we think of the content of the resulting narrative.

When we evaluate the *product* of research, we must ask whether the collection has a real purpose (i.e., it is not just somebody's vanity project), whether it is accessible to future researchers as feasible, and whether all the processes surrounding the interview, the recording and transcription processes, and the plans for archiving the results are as transparent as possible.

5

METHODS

We have been emphasizing the need for a systematic approach in order to elevate everyday storytelling to the level of oral history as a scholarly endeavor. It is therefore necessary to discuss in some detail the methods that underpin this approach. While the interview is the heart of the method, it would be a mistake to assume that conducting an interview is the sum total of the method. Because of its importance, the interview will be treated in detail in a separate section, but first we must make sure to embed it in the larger process that is, properly speaking, the complete oral history method.

Designing and Carrying Out an Oral History Project

Develop Clear, Coherent Research Goals

Do you want to study a particular event or some other collective activity, or are you more interested in individual life stories?[1] If the latter, are you inclined to the "typical" or to the "extraordinary" storyteller? You should have more than personal preference guiding your decision, although you should not discount your personal feelings. Is there some theoretical question in your academic field that can be addressed by using oral history? Is there an issue related to the practice of a professional field that might be illuminated by case material developed through oral history? Is there an external source of support (e.g., a civic association that asks for your help in setting up its own oral history archive, or a local historical museum that wants you to contribute an oral component to complement its visual displays) that guides your choices?

Conduct Preliminary Research

Locate any other sources that might shed light on your chosen topic. These sources may be found in other forms of documentation (e.g., old newspapers, collections of letters, diaries, heirlooms, and/or photos) or in the work of other scholars, including other oral historians. If existing sources tell the whole story to your satisfaction, you might need to reconsider the necessity of choosing a different topic. More likely than not, however, your preliminary research will identify gaps in the record that you can tailor your study to fill. It should go without saying (but I will say it anyway) that your notes from this preliminary phase should be kept neatly, in a place that is easily accessible, and in a form that allows you to retrieve them with ease (i.e., do not use such elaborate codes to disguise identities that you forget the key to your own puzzle.[2]

The exact format for your note taking and storage is up to you. Some people still like to use hand-written notes on index cards or on sheets of paper kept in a loose-leaf notebook, although most people nowadays will transfer the information to their computer. If you use the latter system, be sure to back up your files in some way so that you have multiple copies on hand. The point is that you will be the one using the system, so make sure it suits your needs. A biographical information form, which helps you keep track of your interview subjects, is one common way to make notes; a sample form is included in the appendix.

Define Your Population Sample

If many people are associated with an organization or event, how many interviews will you need to conduct so that you have adequate coverage? The most common seat-of-the-pants rule is to keep interviewing people until you begin to get redundant information. (In cases in which all the participants know each other, it might be necessary to interview all of them just to avoid hurting anyone's feelings, even if you are getting redundant results.) If you are doing a single life history, how will you choose "the one"? Whether you are contemplating one interview or a number of them, how will you approach the person or persons and convince them to participate? Will you need the cooperation of people other then the interview subjects? If so, how will you identify them and how will you convince them to cooperate? There is, of course, no standard answer to these questions—the choices you make will have to be guided by the particular circumstances surrounding your project. The point, however, is that a considerable amount of background research is required so that you can make informed and useful choices. Good oral history does not result from an unprepared interviewer just showing up with a tape recorder on the spur of the moment.

Assemble Your Equipment to Fit Your Purposes

More will be said about equipment later on, but for the moment we can say that recording technology is like any other tool—it is neither good nor bad in the abstract; it is good only to the extent that it accomplishes your purposes. So if you are doing a study involving a school music program and you expect the people you interview to play instruments or sing as part of what you record, you should plan to use equipment with finer recording capacities than would be necessary for recording simple spoken words. If you are going to be the mobile one (as opposed to being in one place and having your interview subjects come to wherever you are), you might need light-weight, relatively easy-to-maintain equipment, whereas bulkier, more complex material might work well in a single setting. Do you need visual as well as audio recording capability? If so, of what quality? (An audio or visual recording that is going on display in a museum will obviously need to be of higher quality than one that is simply used as a source for you when you write your report. Material to be uploaded to a Web site also has specific quality markers that you should be aware of before committing yourself to any particular kind of recording equipment.)

Test Your Equipment and Get to Know It

Like wearing brand new shoes to the senior prom, taking just-out-of-the-box equipment to an interview is a strategy likely to end in tears. Even tech-savvy people will benefit from knowing the quirks of the particular equipment they are using and thus achieving a level of comfort with it. A researcher fumbling with unfamiliar equipment is not a sight that earns the confidence of an interview subject.

Get to Know Your Most Important Piece of Equipment: You

Tape recorders, video cameras, computers, microphones, digital media, and so forth are all necessary adjuncts to the research process. Since oral history, as a special case of qualitative research, is predicated on a highly personal interaction between researcher and interviewee, you are your own most valuable piece of equipment. As such, a little critical introspection is well worth the effort. Reflect on the kinds of situations, settings, or interactions that you feel most comfortable with; can you maximize them in conducting the research? If not, how can you compensate? What kinds of situations, settings, and interactions make you most uncomfortable? Can you minimize them in conducting the research? If not, how can you compensate? Remember that there is a lot you can do to accommodate yourself to the conditions of the research—in terms of both your comfort level and that of the interviewee. Your clothing, hair style, use of jewelry or fragrance, and so forth can all be modified so that you are maximally acceptable to the people you are interviewing. (Of course, you should not make any modifications that you find truly offensive to your own sense of identity or integrity.) There also are some things about you that you cannot do much about (e.g., your gender, your relative age, your perceived racial or ethnic group); if you think these will be a factor in how your interviewees relate to you, can you find a graceful way to put them on the table to clear the air and then put them aside so that they do not become the main focus of attention?

Compile a List of Topics or Questions

You will not necessarily need to create a formal survey/questionnaire—in fact, I would advise against it, as such a format almost certainly leads to a mechanical, third-degree interrogation rather than a more natural conversation that is the hallmark of the oral history style. The list of questions should be for your reference only; it should serve as a reminder to you of the matters you want to be sure to discuss with your subject. The questions need not be rattled off like a checklist, nor should you become attached to bringing them up in any particular order. Your list should reflect what you have learned in your preliminary research. You should not be such a know-it-all that the person you are interviewing feels no need to add anything, but you should be able to ask intelligent questions that show you have done some homework and are interested in learning more.

Develop a Plan for Storage and Retrieval

Even before you begin the active part of the research, have a clear idea about how you will label your recorded material, where it will be stored, who will have access to it, whether you will send copies to the people you have interviewed, who will have the right to determine what is done with it, and what products will result from the project. Consider whether you will have your interviews professionally transcribed and, if so, be sure to include fees for such transcription in your budget. There may also be fees for storing and curating your files, which you should anticipate as you plan your project.

Practice Interviewing

We live in an "interview society" (Fontana and Frey 2005:698). We are saturated with everything from news reports to celebrity-driven talk shows that feature interview formats. As such, we tend to assume that conducting an interview—which is just a formalized conversation, after all—is something anyone can easily do. It's just an extension of what we do naturally all the time and anyway; we've seen it done by the pros millions of times. Right? Not quite. We need to remember that the media models are not entirely appropriate to our purposes, even if we could somehow emulate them. The adversarial, interrogatory approach of the news reporter grilling an errant politician and the softball game of the show biz-savvy host chatting up a celebrity about his or her latest movie are equally inappropriate for our purposes. A more detailed outline of effective oral history interviewing techniques is provided later in the chapter. Try them out with people you feel comfortable with before you embark on your project. As with familiarizing yourself with the mechanical equipment, getting to know your own strengths (and weaknesses!) as an interviewer is well worth the effort. Learn to play to your strengths, downplay your weaknesses, and if possible, work to overcome the latter as you develop your own personal style as an interviewer.

Verify Your Appointments

Make sure that you have set up definite schedules for meeting with people you want to interview. Be very clear about the day, time, and place of your meeting. If you are traveling to meet someone, be sure you know the way and give yourself ample time—it is better to arrive a few minutes early than to keep people waiting, particularly since they are going out of their way to accommodate your research agenda. In the same manner, do not schedule appointments on a very tight schedule; some interviewees might show up late, or the interview itself might run overtime. It is not good practice to keep someone else waiting while you are dealing with another interview. Always have a Plan B when scheduling interviews.

Know Your Surroundings

If you are conducting interviews in your own space (e.g., your home or office), try to look at it with a stranger's eye to see how it can be made maximally comfortable and inviting. Arrange the furniture so that there is not a desk or other piece of furniture forming a barrier between you and the person you are talking to. Make sure that your recording equipment is conveniently, but unobtrusively placed. Consider removing or hiding objects that might be distracting (e.g., put a cover over your giant aquarium).

If you are meeting a person at his or her home or office, take a few minutes to find the most convenient way to place your equipment. Try to stay away from noises that might not be noticeable in person but that tend to be magnified on tape (e.g., ticking clocks, humming ACs). Ask politely that your interviewee keep children, spouses, pets, nosy neighbors, and other distractions away unless there is a clear emergency (or if those others are somehow germane to the story being told). If you are meeting in a public place, be sure that it is a space where you can spend an extended period of time without causing inconvenience to others; it might be pleasant to meet over lattes at the local coffee shop, but not if there is a line of people giving you harsh looks because they are waiting a place to sit. Be sure that the public space is not too noisy. Again, it might not appear so in person, but be aware of how ambient sounds might record on tape. I once conducted a lengthy interview on the lovely, shady veranda of a West Indian home, only to discover when I played back the tape that most of the words had been drowned out by the rustling of the palm trees, so soothing a sound in person, but so grating on tape.

Be Sure the Person You Are Interviewing Understands the Nature of the Project

As academics we take if for granted that everyone knows what "research" entails, but we cannot assume that this is general knowledge. It is a good idea, therefore, to explain in detail what your purposes are, what the procedures will be, and, most important of all, what will happen to the recorded material. As noted above, you should have all these details worked out well ahead of time; these explanations should be introduced when you first set up the interview, and repeated before beginning the interview itself. Do not give your interview subject the impression that you are making things up on the fly. I once made the mistake of omitting this step when interviewing a retired educator, whom I naively assumed would already know all about the procedures for conducting an interview. When I turned on the tape recorder, he insisted that I shut it off; it was his understanding, he said, that this interview would be "off the record" because he was afraid that I would ask him to criticize the administrators of the school where he had worked. He graciously changed his mind once I explained that he did not have to speak about any topic with which he did not feel comfortable, but I could have saved us both the embarrassment had I done so right off the bat. It is also a good idea to make sure that your informant understands any arrangements that might be made for compensation for the interview, as well as for sharing in the proceeds (e.g., royalties) for any products of the research.

Record a "Header"

Before you launch into the interview itself, record an introduction—"This is Michael Angrosino interviewing Mr. John Jones at his home at 2 PM on May 19, 2006, about his experiences with the Special Olympics." You should certainly affix this information to a printed label on your tape or CD, but it is good added insurance to have it on the recording itself.

Engage in Some Preliminary Small-Talk

Unless your interviewee is the kind of person who has made it clear that his or her time is limited, do not jump right into your questions. Rather, create a more natural mood by making casual conversation. After all, you are two relative strangers who will soon be sharing some intimate moments; give yourself the benefit of getting to know each other a little before you plunge into deeper waters.

Be Mindful of Your Body Language

If you are tense and hunch over your tape recorder, you will certainly make your interview subject tense as well. On the other hand, if you are lounging casually and appear to be easily distracted, you will give the impression that the whole interview is a matter of no great importance. Be aware that if you sit with your arms and/or legs crossed you may give the impression that you want to create a barrier between you and the interviewee. Your facial expressions and hand gestures might send messages that appear to contradict what you are saying. ("Yes, your hometown does sound like it was a wonderful place to grow up" is undercut as an affirmation if it is uttered with your eyes rolling and your hand flapping dismissively.)

Leaning forward toward the person you are talking to, by contrast, can convey a message of empathy and interest. Nodding one's head in agreement or affirmation is also usually a good sign (if it is not overdone). Taking the hand of someone who is in the midst of an emotional episode may also be a positive gesture—unless in the context of the interview relationship such a gesture might be misinterpreted as overly familiar, even suggestive. In short, you must be sensitive to the personality and attitude of the person you are interviewing and be ready to respond appropriately to whatever cues are being proffered.

Prepare a Graceful Exit

Once you have completed the interview itself, do not simply turn off the recorder, pack up, and leave. Think of some appropriate ways in which to come to a more comfortable conclusion, particularly if the conversation has dealt with intensely emotional issues. One respectful way to conclude an interview is to ask, "Is there anything we haven't dealt with that you would like everyone to know?" This strategy allows the interview subject him or herself to come to a conclusion and not feel cut off by an impatient researcher. It also encourages interviewees to feel that they are real parts of the research effort; in the current social science terminology, it acknowledges the fact that they have "agency" in the process. Except in very unusual circumstances, do not let an interview run for more than 90 minutes, as you risk trying the stamina and patience of most people. If at the end of that time you feel there is more to be said, arrange for a follow-up interview; do not simply keep going unless your interviewee firmly insists that you do so. In the follow-up interview, briefly recap what went on before, to get your interviewee back into the story.

Make Sure to Obtain a Release

Have the interviewee sign an informed consent or release form before you conclude the interview. (The chapter on ethics provides further details about this process.) This form will allow you to transcribe the recorded interview and specify any other ways in which it might be used for research, display, and so forth. It should also spell out the conditions under which the interviewee will have the opportunity to review the transcript. Your interviewee should be informed if you are planning to turn over transcription duties to a third party. (See Ives 1995; Neuenschwander 1993; and Sitton, Mehaffy, and Davis 1983 for examples of release forms that you can either use as is or modify to suit your own circumstances.) The formal written and signed release should include all the information you have told your interviewee when setting up the interview, but having it in writing is added protection for both you and the person you are interviewing.

Make Field Notes

As soon as possible after the conclusion of the interview, write up a set of notes describing the situation, summarizing the conversation, and reflecting on your experience. These notes are for your own reference and need not be filed or archived with the actual recordings and transcripts, although you should ask the interviewee for permission to keep them on file beyond the period of research, as they might be very helpful to future scholars drawing on your materials. If your notes include observations or analyses that you consider private or sensitive, devise a workable code for yourself and make sure that they are kept in a secure place. It may be necessary to jot down some salient points while the interview is going on, but under no circumstances should you divert your attention from your conversation to the process of writing.

Send a Thank-You Message

Doing so will allow you to acknowledge in a formal way your interviewee's participation. You might or might not be in a position to offer a more substantial gift or compensation, so do not promise anything you cannot deliver. Most people, however, are pleased and satisfied with the simple courtesy of a written thank-you note. (Unless you are interviewing young people, it is probably better to use old-fashioned notes on paper rather than e-mails or text messages.)

Make Copies

If your interviewee has given you personal materials (e.g., photos, letters), copy them as soon as possible if you can safely do so without harming them, and then return them immediately. It should go without saying that such materials should be handled with the utmost care; even if they are not valuable in the material sense, they probably have enormous sentimental value to the person who has entrusted them to you. You should also make copies of all your recordings and of your field notes. Store the originals in a separate place and use only the duplicates as you continue the research. Be sure that the material is stored in a place where they are not likely to be damaged (a damp basement is probably not a good choice), where they can be kept private, but where they can be easily accessed when needed.

Transcribe or Index the Recordings

Making full transcriptions is a very time-consuming task; one professional transcriber of my acquaintance estimated that for even an experienced person, it takes at least two to three hours to produce an accurate transcription of every hour of tape. In some cases, it is necessary for the researcher to be his or her own transcriber; for example, in my study of the program for deinstitutionalized adults with mental retardation, much of what was recorded would have been unintelligible to someone who was not present for the interviews. But given the time constraints, it might be more efficient to have someone else take over the task. Keep in mind, however, that such services are by no means inexpensive. It might be worthwhile to consider whether you really need full transcriptions. It is one of the enduring ironies of the oral history movement that so many of its practitioners have come to believe that the recorded spoken word is not complete unless there is something written down on paper to accompany it.

In fact, unless there is a very good reason for having the words on paper, transcription might well be set aside in favor of a process of *indexing*, which is akin to making an index of a book: key topics in the interview are listed and the place(s) at which they are discussed on the tape are noted. In this way, you can go back to the specific portion of the discourse that you need, instead of wading through the entire tape. If you want to make the occasional direct quote in your report, it is far easier to transcribe just the sentence or two (recovered through the indexing process) than to transcribe everything just for the sake of capturing the several sentences that you want to be able to repeat verbatim. Indexing is not an easy task—it requires a good amount of patience. But it does not require the same sort of technical expertise that a professional transcriptionists has, and it can usually be accomplished by the researcher him or herself in considerably less time than it takes to produce a full transcript.

Whether or not to transcribe videotaped materials is a matter best left to a case-by-case assessment. Many people believe that a videotape can stand on its own as a document in a way that an aural recording cannot (perhaps because, as a culture, we are now far more attuned to TV than to radio when it comes to getting information), but even TV news and public affairs shows routinely allow viewers to order transcripts, so there might be some who expect you to do the same. As with the transcription and indexing of audiotapes, the transcription and indexing of videotapes is a time-consuming and exacting task; if you do not have the time or if you are not confident in your technical expertise, and if you absolutely need the transcription, it might be best to hire a pro, even if doing so can be a costly option. If nothing else, professional transcriptionists are familiar with the necessary equipment and/or software (see comments in chapter 6 on the technology of research) and are probably faster and more accurate typists than you. They may also be more objective when listening to tapes—they are less likely than you to get hung up on what you thought was being said.

Analyze Your Results

There is now an array of software that facilitates the analysis of narrative data so that themes can be conveniently discerned and theories built and tested. (Berg 2004:289–293 is a good place to start learning about such applications, but be aware that technology is rapidly changing so that anyone conducting narrative-based research must constantly update his or her repertoire.) Even if you are analyzing your materials "manually," be sure you have a consistent and transparent method for doing so. Yow (2005:282–310) provides the definitive treatment of how to analyze and interpret oral history interview materials. The kind of analysis you conduct will depend on the final product you envision. Are you writing a research report or doctoral dissertation? If so, your analysis will likely to be shaped by theoretical issues in the current literature. Are you planning popular book? If so, your analysis will probably seek to link your material to matters of interest in the popular culture. Are you contributing to a museum exhibit? If so, your analysis should allow you to present your material in ways that lend themselves to clear visual categorization. Are you creating an archive for a club or organization? If so, your analysis will be guided by the particular areas of interest to that group. Are you making a documentary film? If so, you should be mindful of the organizing point around which everything can be organized. (Films, unlike books, are rarely successful if they try to make too many diverse points.) Are you turning the material into literary stories or fictional films? If so, you will need to figure out which elements in the interview material lend themselves particularly to the telling of compelling stories. Each result necessitates a different kind of analysis. One size does not fit all.

Asking Questions:
The Protocol of an Oral History Interview

As noted above, it is a good idea to have a general outline of topics and issues that you want to cover in the interview, although you should avoid turning this list into a formal survey instrument. It is not necessary to introduce your topics in any particular order, but it is always a good idea to begin with a general question that leaves ample room for an elaborated response. Some discretion is necessary here: do not make the question too general ("Tell me about your life"), since most people will be at a loss as to how to answer, but do not make it so specific that it appears to foreclose anything beyond a narrow range of responses ("What Little League team did you belong to?").

It is difficult to provide absolute guidelines; you will need to "read" your interviewee to gauge the extent to which he or she is comfortable answering different types of questions. As a corollary to this caution, it is probably a good idea to begin with the most neutral topics and work your way to the more controversial or emotionally charged ones. The catch, however, is that it is not always possible to determine which is which; a topic that might seem wholly inoffensive to you might evoke a very strong, disturbing response from your interviewee—and vice versa. Again, you have to develop the skill of "reading" the person you are talking to in order to find where he or she draws the line marking dangerous waters. We do this sort of thing all the time when talking to friends; we just have to learn to do so more quickly when we are talking to someone we do not yet know that well and do not have the time to cultivate for the long term.

Ask Questions One at a Time

Academics are masters of the prolix compound question. Avoid the tendency to frame your thoughts in this manner. Do not put your interviewee in the uncomfortable position of having to say, "I really don't know what you're driving at." Likewise, avoid the academic's tendency (also found among television pundits interviewing politicians) to deliver a lecture outlining and explaining your own position before you get around to asking a question.

Ask Questions that Allow the Interviewee to Elaborate

In other words, avoid questions that can be answered with a simple "yes" or "no." Although the elaborated answer may take you off on what appears to be a tangent, this is a sign of a fruitful interview and not of confusion. If all you get are monosyllabic answers to predetermined questions, there is scarcely a point to doing the interview. Sometimes the most interesting information comes when the interviewee goes in a direction you had not anticipated.

Be Facilitative Rather than Directive

Your questions should enable the interviewee to go off in whatever direction he or she thinks appropriate. On the other hand, if he or she is wandering so far afield that you fear getting completely lost, it is acceptable to gently nudge the conversation back to what you perceive to be the track. This, however, is another one of those judgment calls based on your reading of the interviewee and his or her interests and capacities. Some people are marvelous raconteurs who can be trusted to get to the point eventually even if they seem to ramble; others, however, may be obviously lost and looking to you for guidance. So if you are interviewing Garrison Keillor, the well-known radio host, author, and raconteur, just sit back and enjoy the stories; for other subjects, be alert to the possibility that they might be looking for you to help them get back on track.

Avoid "Leading the Witness"

We are probably all familiar with this phrase from the numerous courtroom shows on TV. "Leading the witness" is essentially putting words in his or her mouth. This is very bad practice in an oral history interview. Do not ask, "How terrible was it to grow up during the Depression?" Instead, get at the same information without prejudging the response: "What was it like for you to grow up during the Depression?"

Be an "Active Listener"

Some celebrity interviewers give the impression that they are not paying a bit of attention to what the movie star on their couch is saying, probably because they already know what he or she is going to talk about. But since a good oral history interview can—and should—go off in interesting and unexpected directions, you must carefully attend to the discourse. Doing so does not require you to stare fixedly at your interviewee. "Normal" eye contact does not mean unblinking focus; in fact, the latter might well be interpreted as a sign of lunacy rather than of caring. In any case, give indications that you are, in fact, listening. Give affirmation every so often (e.g., "Oh, I see," "Yes," "Uh-huh") in the course of a long monologue. Frame your next question in terms of the material the interviewee has brought up him or herself. It is very disconcerting for a person to expound at length on a certain topic only to have the interviewer ask what was clearly the next question on a list, without reference to what has just been said.

Gently Encourage Specificity

Sometimes people settle for generalizations or abstractions on the assumption that you are getting their point. Even if you *are* getting it, you need to clarify it for posterity—others listening to the recording or reading the transcript might not be as clued in. So always be prepared to ask for examples. If, for instance, someone says, "I was in New York on September 11 and it was the worst day of my life," he or she might reasonably expect you to understand why and let it go at that. But your task is then to ask, "Can you tell me some of the things you saw that day that stand out in particular?" Clarification is also necessary when an interviewee gets too specific in ways that the listener/reader could find confusing. For example, someone might say, "The schoolhouse was down in Millerstown." Your job is to politely interrupt and ask, perhaps, "Now where was Millerstown in relation to your home?" Interviewees sometimes give visual examples that do not translate onto audiotape. "Our dog was this big," he or she might say, indicating the size by holding arms outstretched. "Oh, you mean about two feet long?" you could ask. Sometimes it is important to clarify the meaning of unfamiliar terms. For example, in my first encounters with West Indian interviewees, I kept hearing the term "lime." I knew from the context that they were not referring to citrus fruit, but I could not exactly tell what they were getting at. I had to ask them to explain it. (It means a group of people who come together, usually to drink and "hang out.") And sometimes it is simply necessary to ask someone to spell a difficult or unusual personal or place name.

Probe for the Emotional Content of a Statement

An interviewee might think you want just the facts, and while the facts are certainly valuable, you also want to know what the person thinks or feels about the matter under discussion. This, after all, is the great advantage of oral history and other narrative-based research, as distinct from survey or questionnaire research. But do not be satisfied with one-dimensional emotive terms ("I felt sad.") Ask the person to give examples of how he or she behaved when in that condition. Be prepared if such a request leads to some sort of emotional outburst because you cannot always know in advance which topics will and will not be considered sensitive by a particular person. I advise you not to ask in advance about off-limits topics, since your question will only put an interviewee on edge, anticipating some sort of unwelcome line of inquiry. Also remember you are not in the interview in the role of a therapist (even if you happen to have certified counseling expertise in other contexts), and you should not try to "fix" the situation. Simply be a comforting presence until the extreme emotion of the moment passes. Needless to say, if the response includes violence—or even the perceived threat thereof—you are under no obligation to stay. I once had an agitated interviewee throw a Coke in my face; I chose not to take it personally, reasoning that no real harm was done, and we went on and laughed about it later. Had he thrown a cup of scalding hot coffee on me, or if the Coke had irreparably damaged the tape recorder, my response probably would not have been so calm.

Be Comfortable with Silence

Sometimes more is said without words than with them. Be attentive so that you can distinguish a meditative or reflective pause (which you should not impede) from a simple I'm-bored-and-don't-feel-like-talking-any-more hiatus. In the latter case, see if you can steer the conversation back to a place more interesting to the interviewee; failing that, bring the interview to a close as gracefully as possible. In any case, be sensitive to the conversational style of your interviewee and respect his or her hesitations or pauses—you are not obliged to fill every second of the interview with chatter.

Be Real

Some older manuals on interviewing techniques urged researchers to be neutral presences—in effect extensions of their tape recorders. They were supposed to be recipients of whatever the interviewee chose to say and under no circumstances were they to offer commentary other than the occasional, "Uh-huh." On reflection, however, I find this advice to be highly questionable. After all, this is not how we act when having a conversation with a friend. A conversation implies some sort of reciprocity— not a monologue delivered to a blank wall. So it is perfectly appropriate, in my view, for you to offer your own comments, perhaps telling an anecdote from your own experience that complements something the person has just told you. You should not, of course, hijack the interview by turning it into an account of your own life and times, but it is fine for you to share something of yourself, as doing so gives your interviewee a sense of talking to a real person rather than to a machine. I would also go so far as to say that if something comes up to which you strongly object, or that you find offensive, you can make your feelings known. You do not need to get ugly about it, but it is better for you to gently express your opinion than to seethe about it and build up resentment against your interviewee. If your expression of an opinion turns off your interviewee, so be it. Only you can decide where to draw the line between "saving the research" and saving your own sense of integrity.

Evaluating an Interview

Keeping in mind the criteria for assuring the reliability and validity of your research as suggested by Moss, the following checklist might prove useful as you analyze and evaluate your interviews. Ask yourself:

- How did I choose the person to be interviewed? Were the people I interviewed the right ones for my research?

- How did I prepare for the interview? Was my preparation adequate? Was there anything else I could have done? Was there any aspect of the preparation that seemed unnecessary in retrospect?

- What kind of equipment did I use? Did it work satisfactorily? What modifications, if any, should I make?

- What kinds of questions did I ask? Which ones worked well? Why? Which ones were problematic? Why?

- Where did I conduct the interview? Did the environment affect the course of the interview? If so, how?

- Did my subject seem eager to talk? How did I encourage conversation?

- When did I tell my subject the purpose of the interview and how it would be used? Did my plans for the research seem to matter to the subject (or did he or she agree to be interviewed just to be polite)?

- Insofar as I could validate them through other sources, how accurate were my subject's memories? How accurate was the subject's reporting of his or her memories? Does it matter?

- How did I feel during the interview (e.g., in control, at a loss, threatened, etc.)?

- How did the subject seem to be feeling during the interview (e.g., at ease, uncomfortable, bored, etc.)?

- Did I learn anything in this interview that might lead me to rethink my original research plans? If so, how can I modify those plans?

- Who is responsible for transcribing and/or indexing? What editing standards are in force? How can I assure the accuracy of the transcriptions/indexes whether I do them myself or turn them over to someone else? Why did I choose to transcribe or index?

- Do subjects have the option of reviewing the tapes of their interviews? The transcripts? Both? If so, are there any limits as to how much they are allowed to modify the material? Do they get copies of the final product?

- Who owns the interview and who has the right to decide how the completed record will be used? Who will own the copyright or otherwise determine how/when the material is published or distributed (e.g., on the Internet)?

Notes

[1] Life history interviewing may make use of the genealogical method (see, e.g., de Roche 2007), but some people choose not to include genealogical material in their narratives, either because they do not know or are not close to their families. Sometimes they prefer to understand their life experiences as independent of family influences. It is therefore unwise to encourage an informant to dwell on genealogical details, although it is certainly a good idea to follow such leads if the person brings them up spontaneously.

[2] A code may be as simple as inventing aliases or numerical designations for the people involved in the project. If circumstances warrant, it might be advisable to write one's notes in a language other than the one spoken by participants. Some researchers might want to use some sort of indexing system; for instance, they might designate a topic (e.g., family relations) by the letter "A," which would appear prominently in margins throughout the notes whenever that topic is raised. A code essentially serves two purposes: to help disguise sensitive material and provide for informant confidentiality (refer to the chapter on ethics) and to provide you with a convenient shorthand key in cases where you end up with copious notes. The precise nature of the code is less important than the fact that it serves these purpose and that you find it easy to remember and use efficiently.

6
TECHNOLOGY

I suppose that somewhere out there one could find an oral historian who is also a whiz at shorthand and who manually records the interview as it is going on. But I have never met such a person and, to be frank, I do not think that this form of recording is a good idea even if it were feasible. After all, writing on your pad requires you to lose far too much eye contact and keeps you from being an active participant in your conversation. So, from the Depression-era projects to the present, oral historians have relied on one generation after the next of audio recording technology. I am old enough to remember when the standard tape recorder used for field interviews was a reel-to-reel model the approximate size of a piano, often supplemented with outsized microphones that needed tables of their own. There are now, of course, many different makes of portable audio recorders, and choosing among them will depend both on your budget and your research goals. Since this technology, like that of analytic software, is changing very rapidly, I will not make specific recommendations here as they will probably be out of date by the time you read this volume, but I will provide some general pointers for your decision-making process.

Most of the older analogue formats for sound recording (e.g., cassettes, not to mention reel-to-reel) are being phased out by manufacturers; it is becoming increasingly difficult to find replacement parts, and their use in new projects is probably not advisable. Many oral historians are now turning to minidisk (MD) recorders, which are portable, mostly hiss-free, come equipped with index trackmarks (which saves you from having to do manual timing if you are indexing your tape), and are not prohibitively expensive. At present, however, those who use the MD format are copying their recordings onto a CD-R (preferably gold rather than silver) or a DVD-R, which are regarded as more long-term archival media, particularly as it is likely that MD will be replaced by newer technology (such as the "flashcard" or "solid state" digital recorder) within the decade. It is probably also advisable that you back up your audio files onto a computer system. Fully digital audio recorders are also now available and have been adopted by journalists, police officers, lawyers, and other professionals, as well as researchers. Such devices plug into computers and upload all recorded information directly to the computer.

Most tech-savvy oral historians advise using external microphones. I was trained in an era when external microphones were huge and clunky and served mainly to intimidate the interviewee (or force him or her to stare at it in fascination at the expense of the interview itself). This situation has changed considerably for the better. Nowadays, for one-to-one interviews indoors, the recommended microphone is a small tie clip or lapel model. If your recorder is stereo and has two microphone sockets you can get two microphones—one for the interviewee and one for yourself. They can be attached discreetly to one's clothes and give good results. For outdoor interviews, a unidirectional (or cardioid) hand-held microphone is best as it will pick up less unwanted noise. MP3 players (such as iPODs) may come with microphones, either external attachments or built into the device. MP3 players allow users to hold and play music and video files, and some can serve as storage devices for computer files. Your choice of a device will depend in large measure on whether you need something strictly for recording, or whether you need additional functions. The Vermont Folklife Center (http://www.vermontfolklifecenter.org) provides a comprehensive Digital Field Recording Equipment Guide that is updated on a regular basis. It is an excellent resource for helping you decide on the kind of equipment that is right for your purposes.[1]

Oral historians have long resisted the temptation to add video to their repertoire, but as the price for video equipment has fallen and as formats such as digital video (DV) have become commonplace outside the research setting, resistance has mostly disappeared. However, even if video equipment is affordable and easy to use, it should not be deployed indiscriminately. For some people, knowing they are being seen as well as heard is still somewhat off-putting; they think they have to "dress up" for the interview. Video also compromises the intimacy and potential for anonymity of the one-on-one conversation that has always been the hallmark of the oral history style.

Video is useful, particularly if one is interested in a visual display (as in a museum or on a Web site). For example, the U.S. Holocaust Memorial Museum's oral history collection contains over 9,000 audio and video interviews with Holocaust survivors. The general public, students, and researchers can see and hear the firsthand accounts of people who experienced, witnessed, or perpetrated the events of the Holocaust. (For more information, go to http://www.ushmm.org/research/collections/oralhistory.) Video can also be useful in pedagogical situations, as it allows for an interview to be reviewed and critiqued in full (i.e., for all the nonverbal elements of the interview that are not captured on audio tape).

The Internet has numerous Web sites that can be useful to oral historians. The Smithsonian Folklife and Oral History Interviewing Guide is now online; it is a solid, reputable resource and the Web site, linked as it is to a major national institution, is unlikely to disappear into cyberspace. The Oral History Association (in the United States) and the Oral History Society (in the United Kingdom) also have Web sites that provide detailed guidance about conducting interviews, choosing equipment, and dealing with legal/ethical issues; both of them are, like the Smithsonian site, likely to stand the test of time. (See the references section for additional Web sites.)

It is always best to do a search of your own to find sites that are active and that pertain to your particular needs and interests. A simple Google search of "oral history" is likely to yield sites that provide how-to instruction, as well as others reporting on recent scholarly work in the field. There is free software available to edit digital audio recordings.[2] A word of caution, however, is in order whenever you purchase, download, or post material involving the Internet. Viruses, worms, spyware, and other works of evildoers can harm your computer and even result in identity theft. Whenever you post anything to the Internet, including audio files, you are giving third parties access to your material, which they may capture and manipulate for their own purposes, regardless of your own original intent. Oral historians should, of course, make ample use of the many and varied resources available online, but due diligence is definitely the order of the day.

Notes

[1] It is interesting to note that they have phased out their section on analog equipment, although they do maintain a link to archived material for the benefit of those who still use that older technology; buying new analog equipment—even if you can find it—is obviously not advisable.

[2] A free Windows-based utility, VoiceWalker, enables the researcher to transcribe digital audio by using a personal computer without any of the more traditional transcription equipment. The original source for downloading VoiceWalker is www.linguistics.ucsb.edu/projects/transcription/tools.html. If you want to invest in your own transcription equipment, however, you will need a basic transcription machine, plus headphones and a foot pedal (which starts and stops the playback). Sony, Olympus, Lanier, Sanyo, and Panasonic all make Micro Cassette equipment. Philips, Dictaphone, and Sanyo also make equipment for Mini Casette systems. If you prefer to hire a professional transcription service, a good place to start is the Tape Transcription Center (http: //www.ttctranscriptions.com). They accept analog, digital, and Web-based materials and return them in e-mail, diskette, paper transcription, or CD-ROM formats depending on your needs.

7

ETHICS

All research undertaken at research institutions in the United States that receive federal funding (which is most of them, either directly or indirectly) is expected to meet federally mandated ethical standards, the guardian of which is the network of Institutional Review Boards (IRBs). IRBs are particularly concerned with informed consent and with the guarantee of privacy/confidentiality. *Informed consent* refers to the degree to which a prospective research subject understands all that might be involved in the research project.

The federal guidelines have long used the term "human subjects" to describe volunteer participants in research projects. Some members of the research community object to the term because "subject" seems to imply that these people are in a position subordinate to the researcher. That relationship may well have been operative in older research studies, but it is no longer considered appropriate. The term "collaborator" is therefore preferred in some quarters, since it suggests that the research emerges out of a kind of partnership between professional researchers and the people they study. Of course, "collaborator" is a word with its own very heavy connotative baggage, but it has the virtue of expressing the hope of a reciprocal partnership in the research enterprise that many contemporary researchers find appealing. However, since "subjects" is so firmly enshrined in the

statutory language, it will be used here, but only with the understanding that no assumption is being made about the relative sta-
tuses of researchers and the people they are studying.

In any case, a person invited to participate in research should
know what is involved and what the projected end product(s) of
the research will be. It is understood that some outcomes are
unpredictable, but a person should be given as much information
as possible before deciding whether or not to join a study. The situation is considered to be analogous to that of a hospital patient
who is entitled to know all the pros and cons of a medical or sur-
gical intervention before signing a permission form allowing the
staff to proceed.

Privacy refers to the desirability of keeping participants anonymous, usually by using codes or pseudonyms. In cases where
doing so is impractical (e.g., a life history project involving only
one person who happens to be a well-known public figure), the
interviewee should be informed that his or her identity will not
be kept private; his or her decision to continue participation will
then be based on this additional information. *Confidentiality* refers
to the means taken to insure that files, notes, and other records
associated with a research project (most definitely including the
tapes and/or transcripts resulting from an oral history project)
are not open to unscreened public scrutiny. The potential research
subject should be allowed to stipulate the degree of confidentiality he or she expects as a precondition for participation.

The issue of privacy and confidentiality is always a delicate
one, but it becomes especially complicated when visual media
are used in recording personal data such as a life history. It is, of
course, technically possible to disguise someone speaking on
video, but the use of voice distortion, pixilated images, or even
the old-fashioned black-bar-across-the-face tends to make the
subject seem ridiculous, more like a figure in a bad spy film or
porno tape than someone participating in a serious scholarly
endeavor. In any case, researchers should take pains to explain
the product of a video recording, just as they have always
explained the nature of the audiotape product. If the potential
subject objects, he or she may suggest ways to alter the recording
so as to preserve privacy; if the suggested editorial maneuvers

are acceptable to the researcher, then the release form should stip-ulate the terms of agreement. If not, the researcher should respectfully step away.

People nowadays are used to being recorded either aurally or visually, and relatively few people object to being recorded sim-ply out of shyness or modesty. So if there are objections to being recorded, they usually have to do with the publication of sensi-tive material that could get the subject, the researcher, or various innocent bystanders in trouble. One possible resolution might be to have the recordings sealed in archival form until a legally spec-ified date (presumably after the parties who might be offended have passed from the scene). This approach might, however, be impractical if the project calls for some sort of immediate product (e.g., a documentary to be aired to celebrate an important anni-versary or, closer to home, a paper due to your instructor at the end of the semester).

Careful researchers should note that even if a subject is per-fectly happy spilling the beans about him or herself and others, those others might be highly offended. Researchers should try as best they can to encourage their subjects to delete material that might be construed as libelous. On the other hand, there is no way to predict with certainty what people will or will not find objectionable. In our society, anyone can sue anyone else about any matter, even if grounds for successful litigation are absent. The best we can hope for when working with material of a sensi-tive nature is to strike the most careful possible balance between what truly does need to be preserved for posterity and what is pointlessly hurtful.

The claim alluded to previously, that oral history is not really research and should thus be exempt from IRB oversight, is not a tenable one. While oral history is admittedly "nonscientific," it is nonetheless research as it is a process of systematic information gathering, analysis, and storage. Moreover, although an oral his-tory interview is unlikely to result in physical harm, it does have the capacity to be emotionally and psychologically impacting. As such, people who participate in such interviews are just as much at risk as are participants in biomedical research. They are, after all, sharing highly personal information that will reach some

wider community in ways they may not have previously anticipated. For all these reasons, it is imperative that whatever else we
might think about the status of oral history research, any project
involving the oral history method should be subject to the most
stringent review to insure that participants are fully informed
about their rights and that their confidentiality is maximally
respected. Bruce Berg (2004:43–74) provides a thorough review of
the history and functions of IRBs and related issues as they pertain to qualitative research in general. Jennifer Howard (2006)
reviews the recent tensions between oral historians and IRBs.

Despite the bureaucratic uncertainties, we can say with
some confidence that the ethical conduct of oral history (whether
or not one calls it research) should involve the following important points:

- **Interviewees must be made fully aware of the goals and
  objectives of the project.** An *informed consent form* should
  be prepared, spelling out these terms; it should be couched
  in readable English (and translated into the research subject's own language, as appropriate), avoiding complex
  legalistic, and/or academic jargon. The form should have a
  space for the subject to add his or her own stipulations. An
  interviewee has an absolute right to refuse to discuss certain issues, to seal portions of the recording (and/or transcript), and to remain anonymous. An interviewee should
  also be informed of his or her right to withdraw from the
  project at any time. When both parties are in agreement,
  they should sign the form; both the interviewer and the
  subject should retain a copy, and additional copies should
  be on file. An informed consent form is not a guarantee
  against a lawsuit, but it does go a long way to establishing
  the good faith of the researcher should a disgruntled interviewee decide to sue. A project proposal that is required to
  undergo IRB review will almost certainly have to include
  samples of informed consent forms. (Projects undertaken
  strictly as course assignments may be exempt from IRB
  review or eligible for expedited review, but it is always best
  to check your institution's policies before assuming that
  you do not have to undergo review at all.)

- **Interviewees must be allowed to respond as freely as possible.** As noted above, the researcher should avoid "leading questions." The researcher is also obliged to create an inclusive and noncoercive atmosphere in which to conduct the interview. The interviewer needs to assure participants that their identities as well as any material by-products of the interview will be kept confidential unless the informed consent form (or a separate release addendum) explicitly authorizes otherwise.

- **Interviewees have a right to enter into an agreement with regard to royalty payments.** In the event that the product of the research is one that can reasonably be expected to earn money (either ongoing royalties or one-time flat fees), arrangements for the distribution and disbursement of funds must be included in the informed consent form. The researcher must stipulate what aspects of the project will be made public and in what format they will appear. Arrangements about copyrighting material should be decided beforehand.

Please note that the Oral History Association has compiled a comprehensive guide for evaluating oral history projects and, more to the point, for establishing standards for ethical oral historical research. (See Oral History Association 2000.)

8

PRACTICING ORAL HISTORY

As we have seen, oral history is a method of systematic data collection and analysis. It relies on, but is not the same as ordinary conversational techniques. As such, it is a method that requires practice and training even though it is a method that can ultimately be taken up by a wider variety of people than can access more conventional means of historical and social scholarship. Oral history is also an interactive process. Its product is dependent, in large measure, on the relationship between the researcher and the person(s) interviewed. Getting to know yourself—your preferences, your strengths and weaknesses—is an essential foundational step in making yourself an effective oral historian. In this chapter, you will be able to explore for yourself the ins and outs of designing and conducting a piece of original oral history research.

With the general principles, theories, methods, and ethical considerations of oral history in mind, you are now ready to begin putting what you have studied into practice.

Step 1: CHOOSE A TOPIC

You should certainly select something that interests you, as you do not want to spend excessive time and energy on material that you find boring or trivial. On the other hand, make sure it is not something that interests *only* you. A good oral history topic should be one that allows people to tell detailed, interesting stories that other people will want to hear about. Even if it is something very specific, such as your grandmother's experiences as a teacher in a one-room schoolhouse, it should be a story that has resonance beyond the confines of your immediate family. What, for example, would such a story contribute to our understanding of the evolution of education in the United States? How might it help us see the demographic trend away from small rural communities to large urban ones? What might it have to say about changing views of childhood or about changing ideas about suitable careers for women?

A topic may be selected using the following criteria singly or in combination:

- **Proximity and feasibility.** You may have a deep and abiding interest in the experiences of people in Papua New Guinea since that land gained its independence, but if you are planning a project that is to be completed in a few weeks while you are taking other courses, this might not be a wise choice as a topic. Find instead a topic of local interest and importance that involves potential interview subjects to whom you have reasonably easy access. You may choose an event with a focus on those closest to you, such as "How My Family Celebrates Kwanzaa." Such a topic has obvious, wider relevance as well, since even if not everyone celebrates Kwanzaa, almost everyone celebrates something during the "holiday season," so they can relate to the general theme of the story. Even if the story seems new or foreign, sharing it may be a good way to inform a wider audience in such a way as to broaden their horizons.

  At this stage of the game, you might do well to avoid topics that are very controversial; learn the basics of the craft first and then start exploring more difficult terrain. Try to strike a balance between a topic that is too broad and generic (e.g., "experiences of immigrants") and one that is too narrow and particular (e.g., "how members of my family reacted the day I broke my toe"). A good approach is to start with something you personally have experienced that you find worthy of more than passing note (e.g., "My physics professor is a woman; until recently there weren't many women in that field.") and then see if you can make a more general social or cultural statement about it (e.g., "What have been the experiences of women entering the 'hard science' professions?") If you can make that transition, you have defined a good topic for an oral history project (e.g., interview several women scientists either at your academic institution or in local industrial settings).

If you are stumped, check your local newspapers to get ideas about "human interest" stories that people seem to be talking about. Local TV news programs are full of such feature stories that allow reporters to put the faces and voices of "real people" to significant events. A station in my viewing area has been running a very effective series of interviews with "hard to place" young people who recount their experiences in foster care and talk about their lives once they have finally been adopted.[1] Or you can think of a theme that relates to something you are studying in one of your classes; for example, if you are learning about "globalization" you might want to find out how local entrepreneurs manage their supply chains in an era of instant communication. Or think in terms of some group to which you belong (school, religious institution, social club, etc.); at least one of these groups might be very happy to have someone help record its history.

In general, it is easier to start with something small and local that can be shown to have wider relevance than to start with a huge and obviously important issue that cannot readily be studied given your time and resource constraints. Studying globalization through local business people is doable; studying globalization by following the processes of merger and acquisition among multinational corporations is not. Keep in mind that a theme such as local entrepreneurs in an era of globalization could certainly be studied by survey methods that yield quantifiable data. But oral history aims to get at the "story behind the story"—in other words, to discover from the lives of real people the bare bones statistics that identify an issue.

- **Decide on your unit of analysis.** Do you want to do multiple interviews with several people speaking about a single focal event, or would you prefer to work with a single informant? If the latter, would you prefer to work with an "ordinary" person whose life somehow seems to reflect some sort of "typical" situation that everyone can relate to, or with an "extraordinary" person (e.g., a leader in the arts, politics, religion, etc.)? Your response will still depend largely on the criteria of proximity and feasibility, but you should also be open to other possibilities: how can I be most effective in using my research to help answer a question or solve a problem that is in the news or that I am learning about in one of my classes?

Step 2: FORMULATE A RESEARCH PLAN

A major scholarly effort, such as a dissertation project or a piece of funded research, will, of course, be accompanied by a major proposal. For the purposes of this book, however, a simpler process is in order. But even so, it is not acceptable to jump into research, no matter how apparently simple and close-to-home, without having a carefully thought-out plan of action. Even a small-scale, modified statement of a research plan should include the following elements:

- **Write out your topic or theme in the most concise possible form—no more than two sentences if at all possible.** For example, "I plan to use the oral history method to study the development of service learning at my university. 'Service learning' is defined as a process of engaging students in meaningful service to their school and/or community through the application of academic skills to projects of need in the community."
- **Establish your unit of analysis.** For example, "I will conduct interviews with five students, five instructors, and

five community leaders who have been involved with service learning projects since the program was initiated at our school." If necessary, you may want to justify your selection of a unit of analysis. In the sample case, you could probably answer many of your main questions by interviewing just the dean or department chair who inaugurated the program. Why, in this hypothetical case, might it be preferable to do more wide-ranging interviews?

Keep in mind that in this sample case, the interviews will be of the traditional "oral history" type; they are not "life histories," since we presumably do not want every detail of everybody's life—just the ones that bear on their participation in this particular program. Also keep in mind that in qualitative research such as oral history, we need not be overly concerned with creating a "representative" sample since we are unlikely to be doing statistical analysis of the resulting information. The total size of the interview population will be guided by considerations of feasibility (e.g., how much time do you have?), but you still must convince others that your sample will be large enough to touch on all the main aspects of the issue.

I have set this case up so that each of the three primary groups involved in the program is given equal weight (i.e., five interviews for each category). It is, however, quite possible that other situations would permit an unequal weighting; for example, a subtle shift in the basic statement in this case ("I plan to use the oral history method to study student responses to the service learning program on our campus") would lead you to interview more students and fewer faculty and community leaders.

• **Specify the logistical parameters of the project.** Where will the interviews be conducted? What is the time frame or calendar indicating the sequence of the main actions involved in the project? What equipment will be needed? Do you already have access to the equipment? If not, do you plan to buy, rent, or borrow it? What other costs might be incurred (e.g., buying lunch for your interview subjects,

paying for transcription or for storage/curation)? From
what source(s) will you fund your project? Will you need
the assistance of others (e.g., transcribers, computer pro-
grammers), and if so, how will you reimburse them for
their services? In all cases, *justify* your choices; you may
want to use the most deluxe state-of-the-art technology, but
do you really need it in order to accomplish your goals?

- **In addition to the resources discussed above, what per-
sonnel resources are of concern?** If you are going to be the
sole interviewer, how do you propose to manage your time
(assuming that you will be taking other classes, working,
taking care of family, etc., while you are trying to complete
this project)? If the theme/topic is large (e.g., a study of service learning at several different schools), it might be a
good idea to consider turning it into a group project; if you
do so, however, you need to specify as carefully as possible
the proposed division of labor. If the interviews are to be
conducted in a language other than English, how fluent are
you in that language? Will you need a translator? If so,
what possible impact might the presence of such a person
have on the research?

- **Give some indication of the wider relevance of your
topic.** For example, is "service learning" being imple-
mented at schools other than your own? If so, what have
experts been saying about the pros and cons of such programs? What do you think you can contribute to the debate
by presenting the voices of some of the people who have
been directly involved? Do you think your school represents a typical approach to service learning, or is it somehow extraordinary in a way that makes it a potential model
for others?

- **Give some consideration to the analysis of the resulting
material.** Do you anticipate using software to help you
analyze your narratives? If so, why? Which one? Justify
these choices. Are you already comfortable using this software? If not, how do you propose to learn it in time to finish your project? If you prefer to analyze the material

"manually" (i.e., without the aid of software), what specific themes or subtopics do you anticipate using to organize the material? To a certain extent, this question is akin to asking you to compose an index to a book you have not yet written, but certainly when writing a book an author has a fairly clear idea about what the main topics are going to be. So too with the analysis of oral history narratives.

Your "index" might change as you gain more knowledge of the subject, but it is always a good idea to go into the project with some notion of the configurations that are likely to emerge from your interviews. As you revise your index, you will also probably revise your thinking about the hypotheses that are guiding your interpretation of the material. Come up with a plan that will allow you to identify and retrieve material to fill in your categories. (You may want to use word-find features in ordinary word-processing software, or you may prefer to use index cards, loose-leaf notebooks, or file folders. There is no one way that is preferable to all others; find the one that works for you.)

Be clear in your research statement about what you are going to do. It is not acceptable to let those reviewing your proposal to assume that you will analyze the data; you must tell them how you propose to do it. Do you plan to transcribe and/or index your recordings? Justify your choice.

• **What do you think your final product will be?** Most of you will be using this book in conjunction with a course, and so your product will likely be a report that only your instructor will read. Nevertheless, try to think creatively about other possibilities for your project. What might you do with the material? Does it lend itself to a paper suitable for a scholarly journal or conference? Could it at some point be expanded into a book? Would it make an interesting focus for a public panel discussion? Would it work as an online document? Does it have a sufficiently visual component to lead you to think in terms of a film or some sort of museum/gallery exhibit? Is the material sufficiently dramatic for you to think of translating some or all of your interviews into short stories, plays, or poems? Opting for any of these alternatives will lead you to some different answers to the questions posed in the previous points.

- **What provisions will you make to uphold the current standards of ethical research?** Consider the concerns that potential participants might have with regard to confidentiality and privacy. You might think that a topic like service learning, for example, is uncontroversial and that most information that bears on that topic is probably already on the public record in some form. As such, you might assume that issues of confidentiality and privacy will be of minor concern. But to the extent that you are asking people to share their personal experiences with this public activity, you are indeed delving into matters that are not necessarily on the record. For example, service learning students might become involved with agencies that, in their zeal to serve their clients, are guilty of technical violations of government funding regulations. Your potential subjects have a right to know what might happen to any insights that they care to disclose in the course of the interview. So even if you think your topic is unlikely to be problematic, go ahead and draft a statement of informed consent that you think addresses whatever concerns (even apparently minor ones) that might come up.

- **Pretest your statement with several people who will not be part of your research project to make sure that it is readable and understandable.** Consider whether you will need to translate the statement into another language. If your informants are children, or are adults who are illiterate (or have a visual impairment), be sure to make provision for having the statement read to them; ascertain whether another person is authorized to sign it on their behalf. Be sure you are thinking not only about the ethics of the interviews themselves but also about concerns that might arise in the analysis phase (e.g., who has access to transcripts?) and in the final-product phase (e.g., if the final product will be a book that earns royalties or a film that earns revenue, how will the proceeds be shared?)

Try to anticipate and justify any need you might have to borrow material (photos, diaries) from your informants and be prepared to specify how you will safeguard that material and the time frame for their safe return. Be sure to keep careful vouchers for all personal property that you have borrowed. If your final product takes the form of some sort of permanent archive, one or more of your informants may wish to make a permanent donation of those photos or other memorabilia. If so, work out a plan to execute a legal transfer of property.

You must also make provisions for how and under what circumstances the public will have access to the material in that archive. Think very carefully about what you can honestly deliver. Do not promise to keep your tapes and notes in a locked vault if you really do not have access to such a thing. Remember that even if you are doing a limited class project for your instructor's eyes only, there is a very strong likelihood that at some point you will be discussing your activities with your classmates; your instructor may even build such discussion into the course. Your informants should know that although such discussion does not amount to "publication" in the strict sense of the term, it does amount to making certain details about their narratives available to a designated "public." They need to be aware of this possibility in advance in order to make a reasoned decision about their participation.

Step 3: DO BACKGROUND RESEARCH

As noted earlier, you want to be as familiar as possible with the topic you have chosen so that you can ask intelligent, meaningful questions. The goal of background research is to prepare you to be a sensitive participant in the conversation; it is not to turn you into such an expert that you really have no need to interview anybody. Depending on the topic you have chosen, your research might lead you to published sources (either scholarly books/journals or "popular" outlets such as newspapers, magazines, or Web sites). In the case of the service learning topic we are using for our hypothetical example, the source material might be in unpublished archives (e.g., course syllabi, memoranda); in this case, such archives should be available for inspection (especially if your school is a public institution), although files belonging to private corporations might not be so easily accessed. If you are dealing with a topic that extends back in time, be prepared to work with archives that are in disarray, in inconvenient (or even unpleasant) locations, or in various states of disrepair.

Step 4: DRAW UP A QUESTION GUIDE

Remember that you are not to compose a formal questionnaire. But you do need an annotated list of topics that you want to cover and points that you want to clarify. The guide is for your convenience only; your interview subject should never have cause to suspect that you are reading mechanically from a prearranged script. Try not to make your guide too complexly detailed, but it should not be so brief as to become cryptic, leaving you puzzled about what you meant when you jotted down that note. It should serve as a prompt for your memory during the interview—it should not replicate the coding scheme you will be using as you analyze the full narratives. Do not worry about whether your question guide meets "approved standards." A guide is only good to the extent that it helps you.

Step 5: PRACTICE, PRACTICE, PRACTICE

Even if you consider yourself experienced and skilled in all aspects of the craft of interviewing, you should still give yourself the opportunity to work out any kinks before you enter the interview. It is essential to practice using your tape recorder, laptop, camera, and other equipment; do not rely simply on a quick read-through of the instruction manual or tips from friends. By the same token, practice the interpersonal aspects of interviewing; set up sample interviews with members of your class or with willing family/friends. Ask them to help you identify both your strengths and weaknesses as an interviewer. Determine whether you can avoid situations in which you think you are weak; if you cannot, how can you minimize the weakness—or improve so that it is no longer a sore spot? Learn to monitor yourself as well (voice too loud or soft? too much jangly jewelry? overpowering cologne?). In all cases, be thoroughly honest with yourself so that you can truly play to your strengths as an interviewer.

Keep in mind that just because you admire another person's interviewing style does not mean that you should adopt it for your own. You must find a style that is comfortable for you—what works for your friend (or for Larry King) may be wholly inappropriate for you. It is always better to be yourself rather than an imitation of someone else, no matter how admirable that person might be. Always remember that oral history is as much an art as it is a scientific practice; it is based on the ability of the researcher to forge a bond with the person he or she is interviewing. Even if that bond is only temporary, it is still a meaningful relationship, and no meaningful relationship is ever the result when one tries to be something one is not.

Step 6: MAKE PRELIMINARY CONTACT

If your "unit of analysis" involves more than one interview subject, you need to compile a list of potential interviewees. Try not to worry about achieving some magic number; strive instead to get enough people to give you sufficient information about the issues you want to cover. There are several ways to come up with a workable study population.

One effective technique is to identify a "key informant"—a person who seems to be both very knowledgeable about your topic, is (as far as you can tell) well connected in the network of people you think you might want to talk to, and, most important, is available to you. Once such a person is on board with your project, you can ask him or her to recommend others who might make good subjects and who are likely to be available and willing to participate. When these others respond favorably to your invitation, you can ask them to recommend others in turn. When your list of recommended subjects begins to show redundancies (the same people keep getting mentioned by everyone you talk to), then you know you have reached a point of sufficiency. If you have chosen your topic carefully according to the suggestions noted earlier, you should have a small and well-defined group of interviewees and should reach a point of redundancy fairly quickly.

Depending on your topic, another way of drawing up a list of subjects might be to work from ready-made rosters. For example, it you are recording the oral history of a club or government agency, then its membership list may either be on the public record or be made available to you. If you are working on a topic drawn from current events, you may want to rely on your own survey of media accounts in order to form your own opinion as to who the main players might be. If you were working on the service learning topic with a focus on your own school, you might already know some of the people involved; if you are working with other schools, you could not necessarily rely on firsthand knowledge of all the participants.

Once you have a list of people you want to invite to be interviewed, you need to be sure that each of them understands the ground rules of the project. A clear, carefully worded informed consent statement must be made available to all potential participants. If someone seems interested on first contact but then balks after seeing the details spelled out in the informed consent statement, do not press the case and hound the reluctant person to agree to the project. It is often the case that when people know that their friends and colleagues are participating they will be more inclined to go along; if for some reason you find some who remain unwilling, you should never try to apply any inducement that might be construed as pressure to get them to comply. Don't worry if you lose a few people from your interview pool; you are only in real trouble if no one agrees to work with you.

Some of the older manuals of oral history methods insist that "first contact" should always be made in writing. A letter (particularly one on some sort of official-looking stationery) conveys a sense of responsibility and authority; it also gives you the opportunity to set out the terms that will be covered in the actual informed consent form at the outset of the project. Calling people on the phone is discouraged unless you can honestly say that your well-known and highly respected key informant suggested that you call to get in touch. Nevertheless, in the contemporary world people are increasingly unused to receiving formal letters; indeed, many people receiving an envelope from someone whose name or organizational affiliation they do not recognize will immediately assume it to be junk mail and discard it. The informality of the telephone call or e-mail message, which might have seemed rude in the past, may no longer be a problem. If you are planning to work primarily with older people, you may assume that they would appreciate a nicely written letter, but feel free to try other ways to get in touch if you think they might be more appealing to your target population.

Another approach might be to have your key informant personally introduce you to the others so that you can make the invitation face-to-face. The only problem with this tactic is that it might prove to be time-consuming or otherwise inefficient to track down several different people in different locations. It also means that you will have to be extra cautious about what you say. A written letter or e-mail allows you to set your ideas out carefully; a phone call gives you the option of referring to (but not reading from) a prepared script. An in-person meeting with a stranger is by nature a more spontaneous encounter, but even as you converse spontaneously you must be sure that you are covering all the main points about the project and the expectations you have about participation.

The bottom line—as it so often has been in this chapter of advice—is for you to be comfortable. Whether you write a letter, fire off an e-mail, make a phone call, or meet someone in person, you need to be sure that you are making the most effective presentation possible. If you write elegantly, then by all means use a letter as a way of introducing yourself and making a good impression. If you are an especially charming, gregarious type, you might do better with an in-person approach. So determine what you think will work best for you; as always, play to your strengths and avoid your weaknesses.

Your task is simplified to some extent if your project is the single life history, in which case you need not worry about coming up with a list of several potential people to interview. On the other hand, if you have pinned your hopes on working with that one special subject and he or she turns you down, you will have to do some radical rethinking of your topic. Even if the subject of your life history is someone already known to you (e.g., your grandfather) and whose good will you can rely on, you might still run into unexpected difficulties. Your grandfather might be perfectly happy to share his favorite yarns with you but he might freeze at the thought of speaking into a tape recorder and having his words preserved "for posterity." So even though he loves you and wants to help you with your project, he might turn you down. At the other extreme, your topic might lead you to someone who is some sort of public figure who is well- known throughout the community; he or she might be delighted to put his or her story on the record—but only if you abide by stipulations so restrictive that your entire project becomes nothing but this person's propaganda piece or canned stump speech. Most subjects will probably fall somewhere in between; you therefore have to be just as careful to explain your purposes and set out your ideas carefully when inviting a single person as you would with multiple people.

Once you have gotten agreements from your participants, you need to set up your interviews, mindful of the pros and cons of various possible locations, times, and other circumstances. You should defer as much as possible to the convenience of the people you want to interview, but don't agree to times and places that are so inconvenient for you that your own life is badly disrupted. Once an interview has been scheduled, both politeness and prudence dictate that you send a follow-up note (or phone message, or text message, or whatever medium works for you) thanking the person for agreeing to work with you and reaffirming the date, time, and place of the interview. Make sure that this note reaches the person in advance of the interview itself.

Step 7: CONDUCT THE INTERVIEW(S)

Refer to the discussion in chapter 5 about asking questions, and try to conduct your interview(s) according to those guidelines. Remember that these statements are meant to be suggestions, not commands. As you become more confident in your own technique, you may want and need to modify the approach to conducting an interview so that it is more compatible with your own way of doing things. On the other hand, don't be too quick to discard the time-tested strategies embodied in this advice.

I think it is particularly important to conduct an honest self-evaluation of each of your interviews. Don't worry if you didn't do things exactly right. As long as you didn't cross the line and do something flat-out unethical, even less than perfect interviews can still yield interesting and useful information. Always be resolved to learn from your mistakes. The point is that unless you are videotaping your interviews (a procedure fraught with technical and ethical problems, as discussed earlier) it is virtually impossible for someone else to appraise your technique. You must therefore be willing to put yourself under the microscope so that you can learn and grow in your ability to conduct meaningful oral history—and any other kind of social research that relies on interviewing to collect information.

If your course instructor (or some other trusted mentor) is amenable, you might want to share your self-evaluations with him or her. While the instructor will not have seen the interview firsthand, he or she can get some idea of your strengths and weaknesses from your own assessment. Some instructors actually want to read full transcripts; my own preference is not to do so, mainly because the transcripts rarely give me the insight I need to help a novice develop interviewing skills. The transcripts may show specific issues in the formulation of questions, but all the other interpersonal aspects of the intimate, conversational oral/life history interview are lost. If the novice is being honest, his or her self-assessment tells me more about the technique and approach than the transcripts ever could.

Follow up each interview with a note/message thanking participants for their cooperation. If the signed agreement indicated that they would see transcripts and/or receive copies of their tapes, let them know when to expect delivery. If the agreement allows them to edit transcripts and/or tapes, remind them of the parameters you have established for doing so, and let them know the time frame to which you need to adhere in order to finish your project. If they are to get copies of any published materials resulting from the project (or be invited to any sort of public presentation relating to the project) let them know the time and circumstances of such events. Let them know of any arrangements that need to be made for the return of photos, diaries, or other materials you may have borrowed from them. It is very important that participants be made to feel that they are, indeed, partners in the research, not commodities to be used solely for the researcher's purpose and then ignored.

Step 8: ANALYZE THE MATERIAL

Even if you have been very careful to specify your methods of analysis in your project statement, you might still experience a sense of panic when, upon completion of all your interviews, you contemplate the task of making some sort of coherent sense out of what is undoubtedly a large mass of highly diverse narrative materials. Even narratives reflecting a single person's life story can be all over the map given the open-ended nature of the conversational interview style.

In your project statement, you outlined the themes that you expected would be prominent in the interviews. Since you almost certainly asked questions that reflected that expectation, there is a very good chance that the resulting narratives do indeed deal in large measure with those topics. On the other hand, some of those topics might have been discussed in unexpectedly great detail, suggesting the need to subdivide the category. Other topics might have been given the once-over-lightly, so that you may end up collapsing a few into a single theme. Keep in mind as well that oral/life history interviews can take on a life of their own; remember that you were advised not to be too hasty in cutting off seeming digressions, which means that you may end up with a fair amount of material that you did not anticipate at all.

I would be quite suspicious of any body of narrative material that conformed exactly to the expectations of the researcher at the outset of the project; that result might suggest that the interviewer was too controlling and directive in conducting the interviews. By the same token, I would wonder at a set of narratives that bore little or no relationship to the initial statement, a result that suggests that the original project was either not clearly formulated or that the interviewer let the interviews go off on too many tangents. The ideal result would therefore be a set of narratives that clearly address the stated topics/themes, but in ways that were not entirely predicted.

Perhaps the first task of analysis is deciding whether you are going to work directly from the tapes (or, preferably, from copies of the master tapes) or from transcripts. The former requires the additional technology that allows you to pause and stop the tapes at frequent intervals without damaging them; the latter requires the intervening step of making the transcriptions. In either case, you should also have recourse to your own notes as a resource for remembering/reconstructing the context of material in the resulting narratives.

Even if you choose to do a "manual" analysis of the narratives (as opposed to relying on software) it will almost certainly be to your advantage to keep your analytical record with the aid of your computer's word-processing function. Doing so will allow you to make corrections, changes, and other edits with a minimum of mess and fuss. If there are several researchers working on a common problem, having the analysis in word-processed form makes for legibility, ease of file-sharing, and multiple commentaries. And to repeat a warning issued earlier: just because you use ready-made analytical software does not mean that all the work is done for you—you still have to tell the program what you want it to look for.

See the appendices in this text for samples of general forms that you might use in your project. See the appendices to Sommer and Quinlan (2002) for additional examples. See also the several appendices to Yow (2005) for examples of forms and procedural check-lists that might be of specific help to you as you try to make sense of your narrative material. See also Redfern-Vance (2007) for a step-by-step example of doing a "manual" analysis.

Step 9: COMPLETE THE FINAL PRODUCT

As noted earlier, the most likely end product of your research will be a paper to be presented to your instructor. Such a paper will probably include your statement of purpose, a discussion of your methods, and a summary of your findings. An academic paper is, in essence, a summary of the project. It may make use of choice quotes from the interviews, but it is essentially a report *about* what was said, perhaps along with an interpretation or analysis of what was said; the complete record of what was said is absent for the very practical reason that a brief paper by definition has no room for much of anything beyond the summary. It is, of course, possible to think in terms of the sort of publication outlet that would allow for a more comprehensive treatment. A book might include extensive excerpts from transcripts, and a project formally archived in a library or museum might make the full set of transcripts available to the public.

For reasons discussed above, however, the actual transcripts do not always make for very enlightening reading. They may arguably be invaluable to researchers, but they are probably full of the sort of careless grammar, odd word choices, puzzling digressions, and generalized hemming and hawing that characterize spoken conversation. Some scholars therefore have decided to edit the transcripts prior to having them published or otherwise made available to the public; they would, of course, only do so with the permission of the interview subjects. Most oral historians would probably agree that editing for the sake of clarity (and for keeping subjects from sounding like ninnies) is acceptable unless a particular subject insists on presenting him or herself to the world "just as I am."

More controversial is the decision made occasionally (e.g., Crane 1987) to edit out the interviewer and present the narrative as a monologue by the subject, almost as if it were a spontaneous autobiography. My personal take on this question is that such a decision is essentially a literary rather than a scientific one, and that it is defensible as such. But if one's main intent is to contribute to oral history as a species of social research, rather than to create a work of art, then the omission of the interviewer is exceedingly problematic. After all, the essence of the oral history (as distinct from an autobiography that truly arises on the subject's own initiative and is completely under his or her control) is that it is a dialogue, a conversation. It would not exist at all without the interviewer and his or her questions and prompts. To pretend otherwise does a disservice to the very nature of the research technique.

A perhaps even more controversial editing tactic is to rearrange the narrative itself. The most common reason for doing so is to clarify the story by putting it into some sort of linear, chronological order. While doing so may well make it more understandable, it does not always do justice to the act of storytelling itself. There is a preference for chronological narratives in our culture in general, and perhaps among professional historians in particular, but we are certainly familiar with storytelling (in books, movies, TV shows, and so forth) that employs creative chronological conventions, such as flashbacks, flash-forwards, foreshadowing, and other such devices. Novelists and filmmakers make conscious aesthetic choices to "fracture" their stories; but even ordinary people, who hardly think of themselves as artists (at least when it comes to something as apparently mundane as telling others about their own lives) can create "fractured" narratives without conscious effort.

In many cases, the "plot" goes off track because the storyteller has forgotten something and then comes back to it later (perhaps because the interviewer has reminded him or her to do so); in other cases, people may rely on an everyday analogue to the literary device of allusion—the remembrance of one thing leads to a memory that seems superficially unrelated, but that has some sort of deep, thematic meaning to the storyteller. (In litera-

ture, the classic example is in Proust's *Remembrance of Things Past*;
the novel's narrator enjoys a pastry, and all of a sudden, the sight
and taste and aroma—the whole sensory array of that apparently
simple act—brings up the flood of memories about his childhood
that fill the rest of the novel.) Putting such stories back in
"proper" chronological order may thus violate the way in which
subjects actually think about the world and their experiences in it.

It should also be remembered when interviewing people
from non-Western cultures that storytelling conventions may not
be based on a linear model at all; they may by tradition begin "in
media res," as the ancients said (i.e., "in the middle of things")
and then add details that preceded and/or followed from that
central phenomenon in order to explain it. Putting such a non-
Western narrative into "proper" chronological order would be a
gross violation of the cultural integrity of the story as it was both
conceived and told. I have long argued that in oral history, the
style in which a narrative is told is just as important as the mani-
fest *content* of the narrative; in effect, the way in which someone
tells a story (or engages in a dialogue) conveys meaning even
when the content of the narrative is unclear, as in my interviews
with people with mental retardation. (See, e.g., Angrosino 1992.
These matters are treated in greater theoretical detail in
Angrosino 1989a.)

In sum, if your object is to produce a standard academic
paper, your main challenge will be to decide which quotes to
draw from the narratives (in which case a well-constructed index
will be of great help) so as to illustrate points you want to empha-
size in your analysis. If your object is to produce something more
substantial and formal, your challenge will be to decide whether
to publish your transcripts as is or edit them; if the latter, how
will you do so? A standard course paper, however, is not necessarily the sole object of oral history research. We have mentioned
any number of alternatives that can supplement the academic
report, including Web sites, articles for popular media, discussion
forums, dramatic renditions (e.g., stories, plays) based on the collected narratives, and (if you have amassed the appropriate material) such things as museum displays or videos. If your object is
to produce something artistic or literary (i.e., that makes

demands that are different from those involved in social research), what aesthetic choices will guide your selective use of the transcripts?

Based on your prior arrangements with your participants, you will need to decide how (or if) to publicize your final report. Will it remain solely in the form of a paper read just by your instructor? If it is to reach a wider public, what plans have you made for its dissemination and for the continued protection of the privacy of your participants? Will your participants be involved in the public presentations and if so, how?

At the close of your project you will be left with the physical evidence of all your hard work: the tapes with their attendant indices and/or transcriptions. What you do with that material must adhere to the agreements you made with your participants as spelled out in the informed consent form. Will all the material be discarded? Will you keep all the material in your own custody? If so, for how long and under what circumstances (i.e., will anyone else have access to them)? Will they be in the custody of others (e.g., your instructor, the university library, a local museum), and if so, what arrangements for access will be made? Will you return them to the participants or share custody with them (i.e., by making copies for them to keep)? Please note that preserving the records of an oral history project typically requires technical archiving skills and resources that most individuals do not have. Your university library can help you make some important decisions about storage and retrieval. See also MacKay (2006) for more detailed technical information about the processes of archiving research.

Step 10: CONDUCT THE SELF-EVALUATION

In addition to the frank self-assessment you conducted with regard to your interviewing technique, you should wrap up your project with a similarly honest examination of the postinterview phases of the research. Some important points to ponder:

- Was your choice of a research focus a reasonable one in retrospect or would you change it now that I have more information?

- Was your choice of a unit of analysis reasonable in retrospect or would you change it now that you have more information?

- Were your analytic methods sufficient? What, if anything, would you change? Comment specifically about your choice of themes/topics as well as about the way(s) in which you discovered those themes/topics in the narratives.

- If you worked with complete transcriptions, were you satisfied with the quality of the written record? What did the written record add to your understanding of the narratives? Did it detract in any way from your understanding?

- Were you satisfied with your choice of final product? If you had it to do over again would you make the same choice? Why/why not?

- Were you satisfied with the final product itself? What do you see as its main strengths? What weaknesses can you discern?

- To the best of your knowledge, were your participants satisfied with the project (including the conduct of the interviews, as well as with the final product)? If so, what did they particularly like about it? If not, what constructive criticism might they give you?

- If your final product involved some sort of public presentation, what was the reaction of the selected public, insofar as you can gauge it?

- What did you learn from this project about the specific selected topic? About the specific method of interviewing as a data collection technique? About the aims and processes of social research in general? About the pros and cons of qualitative research? About yourself? If you feel you did not learn as much as you hoped, try to account for why that might have been the case.

- Do you have any plans to follow up on this research? If so, what would you like to do?

As with the interview self-assessment, this end-product evaluation might profitably be shared with your instructor, who could use it to help you hone your skills. Even if you think you have done a wonderful job, you might welcome some advice about how to continue to grow as a researcher with the foundation you have already set down.

Note

[1] Do keep in mind, however, that children, the elderly, people with mental disabilities, and people in prison are considered especially "vulnerable" under federal guidelines; projects involving such groups will entail especially careful IRB scrutiny.

SAMPLE LETTERS AND FORMS

As noted in the text, there are several letters and forms that you will need to use in the course of an oral history project. The following are examples of the major types of letters and forms; you can modify them to suit the particular situations with which you are working.

Sample Introductory Letter

Department of Anthropology
Anywhere State University
Our Town, USA 00012

September 1, 2008

Ms. Mary Smith
Department of Student Services
Anywhere State University
Our Town, USA 00012

Dear Ms. Smith:

My anthropology class, ANT 000 (Qualitative Research Methods), has been learning about oral history. The course culminates in a research project for which each of us in the class interviews one or more people about a topic, event, experience, or activity. For my semester project I have chosen to study the development of the service learning program at our university. I would like to gather information from students, on-campus administrators, and representatives of community agencies who have been involved with the program.

One of my fellow students, John Jones, has been involved with service learning for the past year. He told me how helpful you were to him and the other students in your capacity as community liaison in the Dean's office. Would you be willing to sit for an interview of 30–40 minutes in which you share with me your experiences with and insights into the program? I would also appreciate your providing me with any nonconfidential records bearing on the program that you might have in your files.

I will phone you next week to discuss your possible participation and to answer any questions you might have. If you decide to participate, we can also set up a day, time, and place to meet for the interview. I am also looking to interview other people involved in the service learning program and would appreciate it if you could provide the names of others whom I might contact for interviews.

I look forward to talking to you and hope I have the opportunity to discuss service learning with you in person.

Sincerely,
Bob Johnson

Sample Informed Consent Form

Department of Anthropology
Anywhere State University
Our Town, USA 00012

I, Mary Smith, agree to participate in the oral history project on service learning being conducted by Bob Johnson, a student in ANT 000. I understand that my participation will consist of:

A tape-recorded interview of approximately 30–40 minutes in length dealing with my experiences with and insights into the service learning program as it has developed at Anywhere State University. Separate written permission will be given if there is a need for one or more follow-up interviews.

The original tapes will be kept in the possession of Mr. Johnson; backup copies will be held by Professor Sue Jackson, the instructor of ANT 000. No one else will have access to the tapes. The tapes will be indexed, but not transcribed. Mr. Johnson's project will result in a paper to be submitted to Professor Jackson; he will also discuss his findings in a brief in-class presentation attended only by other members of ANT 000.

I give Mr. Johnson permission to use my real name when discussing his findings in his paper and in-class presentation.

Prior to Mr. Johnson's presentation, he will give me a copy of my own interview tape and a draft of the final course paper, in sufficient time to make any suggestions for corrections that I deem appropriate. Such corrections will be limited to matters of fact; I will not challenge Mr. Johnson on matters of interpretation.

_____

(Mary Smith)   (date)

_____

(Bob Johnson)   (date)

Sample Thank-You Letter

Department of Anthropology
Anywhere State University
Our Town, USA 00012

November 15, 2008

Ms. Mary Smith
Department of Student Services
Anywhere State University
Our Town, USA 00012

Dear Ms. Smith:

Thank you for taking the time from your busy schedule to talk with me about your experiences with and insights into the service learning program at the university. I enjoyed our conversation and learned a great deal about the program. I also appreciate your advice about other people to contact for interviews.

As we agreed, I am enclosing a copy of your interview tape and a draft of my final paper, which is due to be submitted to Professor Jackson on December 10. My in-class presentation on my findings is scheduled for December 5. Please let me know if there are any factual data that need to be changed. I hope you will enjoy listening to the tape and I hope you will find my paper interesting as well.

Again, thank you for your help.

Sincerely,
Bob Johnson
ANT 000

Wording of Possible Exceptions to the Informed Consent Form

(The following wording is adapted from Baum 1977:78.)

If the entire interview is closed

. . . except that the entire tape and transcript shall be closed to all users until _____ (date).

. . . except that the parties hereto agree that the entire tape and transcript shall not be made available to anyone other than the parties hereto until _____ (date).

If the interview is closed, but with permissions possible

The interview tape and transcript may not be made available to anyone without my express permission until _____ (date) after which it may be made available for general research.

The parties hereto agree that the entire tape and transcript shall not be made available to anyone other than the parties hereto until _____ (date) except with the express permission of _____ (name of interviewee or his/her designated representative).

If only some parts are closed

The following transcript pages: _____ and the tape relating thereto shall be closed to all users until _____ (date) except with the express permission of _____ (name of interviewee or his/her designated representative).

If publication rights are to be limited

It is agreed that the researcher will not authorize publication of the transcript or any substantial part thereof during my lifetime without my permission, although he and other researchers may make brief quotations therefrom without my permission.

It is agreed that the researcher will not authorize publication by others of the transcript or any part thereof during my lifetime without express permission.

If the interviewee retains publication rights

I reserve all literary property rights to the interview until _____ (date), at which time these literary property rights shall vest in _____ (name of designated holder of rights).

BIOGRAPHICAL INFORMATION FORM

Name _____

Address (home) _____

_____

Address (work) _____

_____

Telephone (home) _____

Telephone (work) _____

Cell phone _____

E-mail _____

Birth date (day/month/year) _____

Birth place _____

Occupation(s) _____

_____

Spouse/closest living relative/other contact _____

Contact information for above _____

_____

_____

Additional biographical information relevant to the project:

_____

_____

_____

_____

_____

_____

REFERENCES

Angrosino, Michael V. 1989a. Documents of Interaction: Biography, Autobiography, and Life History in Social Science Perspective. Gainesville: University of Florida Press.

Angrosino, Michael V. 1989b. The two lives of Rebecca Levenstone: Symbolic interaction in the generation of the life history. *Journal of Anthropological Research* 45:315–326.

Angrosino, Michael V. 1992. Metaphors of stigma: How deinstitutionalized mentally retarded adults see themselves. *Journal of Contemporary Ethnography* 21:171–199.

Angrosino, Michael V. 1994. On the bus with Vonnie Lee: Explorations in life history and metaphor. *Journal of Contemporary Ethnography* 23:14–28.

Angrosino, Michael V. 1997. The ethnography of mental retardation: An applied perspective. *Journal of Contemporary Ethnography* 26:98–109.

Angrosino, Michael V. 1998a. Mental disability in the United States: An interactionist perspective. *In* Questions of Competence: Culture, Classification and Intellectual Disability, ed. Richard Jenkins (pp. 25–53). Cambridge, U.K.: Cambridge University Press.

Angrosino, Michael V. 1998b. Opportunity House: Ethnographic Stories of Mental Retardation. Walnut Creek, CA: AltaMira Press.

Angrosino, Michael V. 2004. Disclosure and interaction in a monastery. *In* Anthropologists in the Field: Cases in Participant Observation, ed. Lynne Hume and Jane Mulcock (pp. 18–31). New York: Columbia University Press.

Berg, Bruce L. 2004. Qualitative Research Methods for the Social Sciences, 5th ed. Boston: Allyn & Bacon.

94 References

Burroughs, Augusten. 2002. Running with Scissors. New York: St. Martin's Press.

Burroughs, Augusten. 2003. Dry: A Memoir. New York: St. Martin's Press.

Charlton, Thomas L., Lois E. Myers, and M. Rebecca Sharpless, eds. 2006. Handbook of Oral History. Walnut Creek, CA: AltaMira Press.

Crane, Julia G., ed. 1987. Saba Silhouettes: Life Stories from a Caribbean Island. New York: Vantage Press.

de Roche, Constance P. 2007. Exploring genealogy. In Doing Cultural Anthropology, 2nd ed., ed. Michael V. Angrosino (pp. 19–32). Long Grove, IL: Waveland Press.

Dorson, Richard. 1996. The oral historian and the folklorist. In Oral History: An Interdisciplinary Anthology, ed. David K. Dunaway and Willa K. Baum (pp. 283–291). Walnut Creek, CA: AltaMira Press.

Edgerton, Robert B. 1967. The Cloak of Competence: Stigma in the Lives of the Mentally Retarded. Berkeley: University of California Press.

Erikson, Erik H. 1963. Childhood and Society, 2nd ed. New York: Norton.

Fontana, Andrea and James H. Frey. 2005. The interview: From neutral stance to political involvement. In Handbook of Qualitative Research, 3rd ed., ed. Norman K. Denzin and Yvonna S. Lincoln (pp. 695–727). Thousand Oaks, CA: Sage Publications.

Frey, James. 2003. A Million Little Pieces. New York: Doubleday.

Frisch, Michael H. 1990. A Shared Authority: Essays on the Craft and Meaning of Oral and Public History. Albany: State University of New York Press.

Goodman, Amy. 2007. Studs Terkel: Curiosity Didn't Kill This Cat. TruthDig.com, November 14.

Grele, Ronald J. 1996. Directions for oral history in the United States. In Oral History: An Interdisciplinary Anthology, ed. David K. Dunaway and Willa K. Baum (pp. 62–84). Walnut Creek, CA: AltaMira Press.

Henley, C.A. 2001. Good intentions—unpredictable consequences. Disability and Society 16(7):933–947.

Hoffman, Alice. 1974. Reliability and validity in oral history. Today's Speech 22:23–27.

Hoopes, James. 1979. Oral History: An Introduction for Students. Chapel Hill: University of North Carolina Press.

Howard, Jennifer. 2006. Oral history under review. Chronicle of Higher Education 53(12):A14.

Isay, Dave, ed. 2007. Listening Is an Act of Love: A Celebration of American Life from the Story Corps Project. New York: Penguin.

Ives, Edward D. 1995. The Tape-Recorded Interview: A Manual for Field Workers in Folklore and Oral History, 2nd ed. Knoxville: University of Tennessee Press.

Langness, L. L. 1965. The Life History in Anthropological Science. New York: Holt, Rinehart and Winston.

MacKay, Nancy. 2006. Curating Oral Histories: From Interview to Archive. Walnut Creek, CA: LeftCoast Press.

Mandelbaum, David G. 1973. The study of life history: Gandhi. Current Anthropology 14(3):177–206.

Menchú, Rigoberta. 1984. I, Rigoberta Menchú, an Indian Woman in Guatemala, ed. E. Burgos-Debray, trans. A. Wright. London: Verso.

Moss, William. 1977. Oral history: An appreciation. American Archivist 40:429–439.

Neuenschwander, John. 1993. Oral History and the Law. Albuquerque, NM: Oral History Association.

Oral History Association. 2000. Principles and Standards of the Oral History Association (Pamphlet No. 3). Carlisle, PA: Oral History Association.

Radin, Paul. 1920. The Autobiography of a Winnebago Indian. Berkeley: University of California Publications in Archaeology and Ethnology.

Redfern-Vance, Nancy. 2007. Analyzing narrative data. In Doing Cultural Anthropology: Projects for Ethnographic Data Collection, 2nd ed., ed. Michael V. Angrosino (pp. 45–62). Long Grove, IL: Waveland Press.

Simmons, Leo W. 1942. Sun Chief: The Autobiography of a Hopi Indian. New Haven: Yale University Press.

Sitton, Thad, George L. Mahaffy, and O. L. Davis. 1983. Oral History: A Guide for Teachers (and Others). Austin: University of Texas Press.

Sommer, Barbara W. and Mary Kay Quinlan. 2002. The Oral History Manual. Walnut Creek, CA: AltaMira Press.

Starr, Louis. 1996. Oral history. In Oral History: An Interdisciplinary Anthology, ed. David K. Dunaway and Willa K. Baum (pp. 39–61). Walnut Creek, CA: AltaMia Press.

Terkel, Studs, 1974. Working: People Talk about What They Do All Day and How They Feel about What They Do. New York: New Press.

Terkel, Studs. 1986. Hard Times: An Oral History of the Great Depression. New York: Pantheon.

Terkel, Studs. 1993. Race: How Blacks and Whites Feel about the American Obsession. New York: Anchor.

Terkel, Studs, 1997. The Good War: An Oral History of World War II. New York: New Press.

Terkel, Studs. 2000. Coming of Age: The Story of Our Century by Those Who've Lived It. Darby, PA: Diane Publishing Co.

Thomas, William I. and Florian Znaniecki. 1918. The Polish Peasant in Europe and America (5 vols.). Boston: Richard G. Badger.

Thompson, Paul. 1988. The Voice of the Past: Oral History. Oxford: Oxford University Press.

Troost, J. Maarten. 2006. Getting Stoned with Savages: A Trip through the Islands of Fiji and Vanuatu. New York: Broadway Books.

Vansina, Jan. Oral tradition and historical methodology. *In* Oral History: An Interdisciplinary Anthology, ed. David K. Dunaway and Willa K. Baum (pp. 121–125). Walnut Creek, CA: AltaMira Press.

Vaz, Kim Marie, ed. 1997. Oral Narrative Research with Black Women. Thousand Oaks, CA: Sage.

Yow, Valerie R. 2005. Recording Oral History: A Guide for the Humanities and Social Sciences, 2nd ed. Walnut Creek, CA: AltaMira Press.

OTHER WORKS THAT MIGHT HELP YOU AS YOU EXPLORE THE FIELD OF ORAL HISTORY

Allen, Barbara and Lynwood Montell. 1991. From Memory to History: Using Oral Sources in Local Historical Research. Jackson: University Press of Mississippi.

Angrosino, Michael V. 2007. Conducting a life history interview. In Doing Cultural Anthropology: Projects for Ethnographic Data Collection, 2nd ed., ed. Michael V. Angrosino (pp. 33–44). Long Grove, IL: Waveland Press.

Baum, Willa. 1977. Transcribing and Editing Oral History. Nashville, TN: American Association for State and Local History.

Cohen, Daniel J. and Roy Rosenzweig. 2005. Digital History: A Guide to Gathering, Preserving, and Presenting the Past on the Web. Philadelphia: University of Pennsylvania Press.

Dunaway, David K. 1996. The interdisciplinarity of oral history. In Oral History: An Interdisciplinary Anthology, ed. David K. Dunaway and Willa K. Bau, (pp. 7–25). Walnut Creek, CA: AltaMira Press.

Fine, Michelle, David S. Surrey, Tiffany Perkins, and Renaissance School Class of 2000. 2002. Keeping the Struggle Alive: Studying Desegregation in Our Town: A Guide to Doing Oral History. New York: Teachers College Press.

Hall, Jacquelyn Dowd and Della Pollock. 2005. Remembering: Oral History Performance. New York: Palgrave Macmillan.

Jackson, Bruce. 1987. Fieldwork. Urbana: University of Illinois Press.

Kelin, Daniel A. 2005. To Feel As Our Ancestors Did: Collecting and Performing Oral Histories. Portsmouth NH: Heinemann Drama.

Koehl, Laura Ann. 2006. Doing Science: Lessons Learned from the Oral Histories of Women Scientists. Ann Arbor: ProQuest/University of Michigan.

Lanman, Barry and Laura M. Wendling, eds. 2006. Preparing the Next Generation of Oral Historians: An Anthology of Oral History Education. Walnut Creek, CA: AltaMira Press.

Matters, Marion. 1995. Oral History Cataloging Manual. Chicago: Society of American Archivists.

Perks, Robert, ed. 2006. Oral History Reader. London: Routledge.

Riccio, Anthony V., Mary Ann Carolan, and Philip Langdon. 2006. The Italian American Experience in New Haven: Images and Oral Histories. Albany: State University of New York Press.

Ritchie, Donald A. 2003. Doing Oral History: A Practical Guide. New York: Oxford University Press.

Rubin, Herbert J. and Irene S. Rubin. 2004. Qualitative Interviewing: The Art of Hearing Data. Thousand Oaks, CA: Sage.

Walker, Melissa. 2006. Southern Farmers and Their Stories: Memory and Meaning in Oral History. Lexington: University Press of Kentucky.

Wengraf, Tom. 2001. Qualitative Research Interviewing: Biographic Narrative and Semi-Structured Methods. London: Sage.

Wigginton, Elliot. 1972. The Foxfire Book. New York: Doubleday.

Please note:

Oral history project reports literally fill libraries. It would be impossible to produce a complete bibliography of such studies and, given the vast diversity of the materials, futile to attempt some sort of "representative" sample. The interested student, however, is directed to several of the "Recommended Reading" sections in Yow (2005), which come as close as possible to providing references for important, interesting, and illustrative examples of oral history. See in particular the sections on pp. 213–215; 244–248; 276–278.

The following Web sites may also be helpful:

Archives of African American Music and Culture
   (http://www.indiana.edu/~aaamc/)
Digital Story Telling Degree
   (http://www.bsu.edu/cim/storytelling/)
Best of History Web sites
   (http://besthistorysites.net/OralHistory.shtml)
Center for Oral History Tradition (http://oraltradition.org)

In the First Person
(http:www.inthefirstperson.com/firp/index.aspx)
Library of Congress: The American Folklife Center
(http://www.loc.gov/folklife/)
Library of Congress: Using Oral History—Student Lesson
(http://memory.loc.gov/learn/lessons/oralhist/ohstart.html)
University of California, Berkeley: Conversations with History
(http://globetrotter.berkeley.edu/conversations/)

INDEX